MW01671089

Thinking MATH Differently

An Essential
FOURTH GRADE Guide
for
Parents AND Teachers

Also part of the **Thinking MATH Differently** *series:*

An Essential KINDERGARTEN Guide

An Essential FIRST GRADE Guide

An Essential SECOND GRADE Guide

An Essential THIRD GRADE Guide

An Essential FIFTH GRADE Guide

Thinking MATH Differently

An Essential

FOURTH GRADE Guide

for

Parents AND Teachers

PATTI J. DIECK

CHRISTOPHER M. SARLO

ISBN: 978-0-9977892-9-4

Printed in the United States of America

Acknowledgements

To our loving and infinitely patient spouses, **Mike and Janine**, who put up with our late nights (and subsequently grumpy mornings!) Thank you for your belief in us, your constant encouragement…and for keeping the coffee fresh and freely flowing!

We *FINALLY* finished!!!

To **Matthew** thank you for every late night conversation that ended with, "You've got this, Mom." and to **Jared** for letting your Mom be your "everyday hero".

To **Adam and Lucas,** thank you for your unwavering support, and to **Ava and Olivia** for ALL of your love and excitement surrounding "Our dad's book!"

YES! Let's walk the dog and hang out at the park!

To our amazing parents, ***Richard & Janet Petersen and Joseph & Fran Sarlo***, also known as our biggest fans, thank you for always letting us know how proud we make you.

Table of Contents

*NOTE: Please take a few minutes to read "How to Use this Book" before diving into individual math topics. This section contains our recommendations on how to best navigate and use this text, which will ultimately result in maximizing your understanding(s).

Preface

"THIS IS NOT THE MATH I LEARNED! HOW am I supposed to help?"
....Sound familiar??

THE CURRICULUM CHANGES EVERY YEAR! HOW am I supposed to build on and lay new foundations?"
....Sound familiar??

In more than 40 years of combined teaching experience, the first and most-often-asked question we get from parents is, "How can I help my child?"

Colleagues and other teaching professionals also want something that is "timeless": strategies and mathematical instructional practices that both transcend program/curriculum choices and "grow with their students."

With new standards now in effect in almost every state, and similar high standards and teaching methods driving math instruction in the others, this question, and need for mathematical understanding has never been timelier.

This guide will help... IRRESPECTIVE of the curriculum or math program your child, or your school/district employs.

The most important thing today's adults NEED to understand is that we didn't *"learn different math"* than our children are learning...we just *"learned math differently"*. Everything adults understand about how numbers work and how to use them is still the same! Wait, let's repeat that... **Everything adults understand about how numbers work and how to use them is still the same!** The major difference is that we learned "how to do things" with numbers without learning "why to do them". This process led to the memorizing of steps rather than simply thinking about what would make sense. Today's math looks and seems quite confusing to many adults, because teaching *"understanding"* instead of *"memorization"* is not as straight-forward a process. There are additional ideas included in the teaching of each topic, which are there to demonstrate the thinking process. To parents these "extra things" often seem confusing, or even unnecessary. But these ideas are **KEYS** to success....and are all specifically pointed out throughout the lessons in this book. What's most important to remember is that our goal for students today is NOT to simply "get the answer"...our goal is for children to understand the processes that lead to the answers. This understanding is what children are then able to USE when faced with similar problems in the real world.

The good news is that there **ARE** simple and practical answers to the questions of how parents can help and how teachers can impact their students' achievement, and this book contains the ones you can use right now. Each learning standard and concept is explained in real, everyday language...finally putting parents and teachers "on the same page"

...and making this guide the perfect companion no matter which curriculum or textbook children use.

As you navigate through the lessons in this book, please keep this thought in mind:

"We don't REMEMBER how to DO math, we THINK about how to USE math to solve problems."

So who are we??

Our incredible journey to this point began PCC (Pre-Common Core)! We have been teaching a combined total of over 40 years in grades 3 through 6, in Suffolk County, New York: Patti 27 years, and Christopher 17 years. A driving force in each of our classrooms has always been the "process of learning"....teaching students to decide what it "makes sense" to do in problem solving situations, and to "puzzle it out" when they aren't immediately sure. It has always been our personal belief that when students learn what it **MEANS** to perform various tasks in mathematics, and when they are taught these concepts through problem solving, they will inherently **KNOW** what to do and how to do it when faced with similar problems. Taking the focus **OFF OF** *finding right answers,* and putting it **ON** *solving problems efficiently and effectively,* makes math thinkers. Teaching algorithms in our classrooms has always been secondary to teaching understanding of what each operation means at its core. In our experience, students who learn this way are far less likely to grow up and become adults who "don't get math". Quite the opposite is true!

It was these beliefs that led to our in-depth knowledge of the Common Core State Standards for Mathematics, and eventually to our work as writers of New York State's Common Core Math Curriculum. (EngageNY.org). Years prior to the implementation of the new standards, New York State commissioned the writing of a new curriculum; one designed and written to meet the standards. A wise decision, given that ***no commercially available textbooks had as of yet been adequately revised.*** Patti worked as part of the team that produced the grade 4 curriculum, Christopher as part of the grade 5 team. Working with mathematicians and skilled lead writers we helped to craft a curriculum that truly meets the standards, while incorporating the very best teaching strategies.

Our work as consultants and professional development providers was the next logical step, as local school districts suddenly found they needed to provide training for their teachers, who had not learned mathematics this way themselves. To date we have worked with numerous school districts, teacher centers, and yes, Parent Groups! Parents, it seems, are eager, even excited(!), to (finally) learn all of the meaning behind the math they thought was "just a set of steps". The single most-heard comment in all of our parent and teachers workshops is always, "This makes so much sense….I wish we had learned it this way!"

Teaching this way for so many years, and doing so as two of a very few individuals who subscribed to this belief, became increasingly more and more frustrating. We couldn't understand why more teachers did not follow this methodology. We came to understand that a focus on "results" was foremost on most teachers' minds …leading to an overemphasis on procedures and test preparation in most classrooms. What we've realized, and seen demonstrated in the growth scores of our own students, is that our idea of "results" transcends standardized test scores. In fact, the less test prep included in students' daily math instruction, the more they are generally able to demonstrate success and growth on those same standardized tests. As we point out in our training workshops, and as teachers who take those workshops report back to us, it is the *teaching of concepts and the understanding of how numbers work* that yields the best results.

Why did we write this book?

The impetus for this handbook was our desire to help calm the frustration experienced by SO MANY following the implementation of the new math standards. Through our many discussions with professors, administrators, teachers, colleagues, and parents, we learned that most of them have had little or no interaction with math taught this way. Since it's not the way most adults learned themselves, they need to become familiar with the concepts, strategies and vocabulary their children are seeing and interacting with daily.

As two of the writers responsible for the creation the NYS Mathematics Modules (now a National Math Program!) we wholeheartedly believe in the new learning standards. With that said let's outline some pertinent facts that may help you better understand *what exactly is happening*:

- The Common Core State Standards for Mathematics, as well as the new math standards in non-Common Core states, are built on the notion that student **understandings of mathematics** are necessary for finding solutions.
- No matter which curriculum (math series) a school/district uses, there are certain **foundational ideas** they all share. All of today's textbook series were either written or adapted for the same set of learning standards.
- Most problem solving is based on the **use of a model**…children are encouraged to use models to show their thinking. While the models are taught specifically, and one at a time, the big idea is that after learning a variety of models, students will "choose one" that makes sense to them as they work.
- The ultimate goal *is* for students to use "standard algorithms" for the four basic operations (the way we learned!), because standard algorithms ARE easier and

more efficient. The **use of the algorithms** simply comes AFTER the understanding of why they work. Research shows this helps learners remember and use the algorithms more effectively.

- The use of **precise mathematical vocabulary** is a key component to teaching mathematical understanding.
- Modeling and problem solving practice, also known as **application**, have replaced pages of repeated algorithm practice.
- **Fluency with facts** (memorization of addition facts or times tables, for example) is an important component to this learning….it has not been eliminated or replaced.
- Learning **"how numbers behave"** and **"what they can do"** (what today's adults would have learned as the *commutative, associative and distributive properties*) beginning as early as Kindergarten takes students all the way through high school.
- Ultimately if students understand how and why to manipulate numbers, we will **create problem solvers….not "answer getters"**!

What makes this book different?

This book was designed to help you help your children… to take the guesswork out of what each assignment means. Throughout this book you will be introduced to the *big ideas* and main topics studied at each grade level, the *models* used to instruct and foster mathematical thinking for each topic, and the *mathematical vocabulary* used to support learning. You will also learn how each topic relates to grade level learning standards. Finally, this book discusses the *fluency skills* expected to be in place at each grade level in order to ensure success with each concept. All of this information is presented in an easy to follow format that links this new learning to "the way we learned".

HOW TO USE THIS BOOK

This book was written for every adult who has looked at their child's math homework and thought, "HUH?" ...or worse, "Good thing I don't have to pass fourth grade again!"

It was written for every teacher who has looked at today's learning standards and thought, "WHAT do they even MEAN??....Where do I START?"

The truth is that today's assignments DO look and feel very different from what almost every adult was taught and is used to. The good news is that even though it looks so different, it's based on the same principles that the math we learned was built on. **"Math"** hasn't changed...**the way we think about it** in the classroom has. Which means that you already know more about this than you thought you did!

Today's math instruction is designed to "directly teach" students a lot of the things we adults had to figure out for ourselves. Let's look at a simple example:

> If we asked you to add 9 to any number, say 35, you would probably respond very quickly that the answer is 44.
> Now...THINK for a moment about how you did that so quickly. You didn't, we're sure, count on 9 fingers. More than likely you simply added 10 to make 45 and then took one off. You knew you needed the number 1 less than 45 because 9 is 1 less than 10**, and you knew it automatically.**

We're going to go out on a limb here and say that you probably didn't learn this strategy in school. For most adults strategies like this one just developed over time. You probably don't know exactly when you learned that...it's one of those things you do with numbers because **you understand that it makes sense and it will always work.**

THIS is the type of thinking and understanding that's now built into math instruction. Since young learners don't have the experience with numbers we had when we started developing these "makes-sense strategies", they need to be taught how to do it. Teaching children to ***understand and apply the way***

numbers work looks very different than simply teaching them ***what steps to follow***....and THIS is where the trouble starts when it comes to helping children with math assignments. This is also where the stumbling block lies for many teachers. Most of today's teachers learned math "the old way" and so it makes sense to them to teach it that way. They recognize the importance and effectiveness of "this new way" but since they didn't learn this way themselves it's not a simple shift!

So what will you find in this book?...

...Everything you need to understand fourth grade math!

Each section of the book represents a major topic of fourth grade math. Within each section are all of the concepts related to that topic, along with the learning standard related to each one. Each standard is explained in **regular "everyday" language**, and is followed by an example. You simply find the concept your child is working on and read the description to understand what the assignment is about. *At times you may need to check out more than one section.* We suggest referencing your child's classwork and then finding the "match" in this book.

We suggest reading through each entire topic, organized as individual chapters, first. Although you may be looking for help teaching or working with one specific concept, it is VERY BENEFICIAL to see how that topic fits into the entire progression of how it is taught. When children are struggling it is often useful for them to see problems presented in alternate or simpler forms. Bringing them "back" to a strategy they have been successful with and showing them how it relates to their current work helps children see the big picture of how it all fits together. It reminds them that they can use what they do know to figure out what they don't. Understanding how each concept "fits" with the others in the topic is what gives adults the insight they need to help it all make sense to children....our prime objective!

The Joys of Problem Solving

Questioning

In addition to the information in the rest of this book, it is also of pivotal importance that you understand the value of asking questions as a way to help your children solve math problems. (Rather than being the source of the answers.) This trains them to think through problems **before** looking for outside assistance. Answering children's questions WITH questions begins in Kindergarten, but becomes much more prominent as children move to later grades. Some problem solving questions may include:

- Do you know the total? (If so then you wouldn't add or multiply.)
- Can you draw a picture? (If so draw it! – "visual representations" often help the problem "make sense".)
- What is happening in the problem/story? (What's the ACTION?)
    - Is there something that is increasing? Decreasing?
    - Does someone/something have more? Less? How much more/less?

The more questions you ask children, which lead to discovering a solution pathway, the better. As parents ourselves, we know that it is MUCH easier, and INFINETLY more efficient, to say something like "just add" or "just subtract". The questioning, however, helps to build conceptual understanding, confidence, independence, and schema.

Asking questions also begins to engage your child in the necessary *internal dialogue* (in their own heads) of problem solving (think about when you try to solve something new, do you often "talk yourself through it?") We want children to develop their own personal strategies for tackling word problems. Whatever their preferred way of doing it is, it MUST make sense to them…MUST be something they can visualize and then puzzle-out….even if it appears to be "the long way" or "more involved" than necessary. Eventually children will develop all of the mental shortcuts we adults employ, but for now letting them develop is the important thing.

"Key Words"

When solving word problems with your child, try to refrain from pointing out "key words" (words that SEEM to suggest a certain operation). Many adults were taught to look for these words as a first line of attack when solving word problems. The trouble is that these don't always work! Let's look at an example:

> Sam found 15 shells at the beach. He found 9 **more than** his friend Jack. How many shells did Jack find?

Of course, in this case, the answer is 6 shells.

It's common to teach children that the words "more than" suggest a subtraction problem, as we see here. Many children are (mistakenly) taught that when a problem states one number is "more than" another, they should find the difference between the numbers....subtraction.

But let's look at another example:

> Sam found 15 shells at the beach. Jack found 9 **more than** Sam. How many shells did Jack find?

Most adults can "see" the action happening in this problem, and "just know" that the answer is 24. But for children who have been taught to "do what the key words say to do" this is a very confusing problem. It is very difficult for elementary children to both follow the problem solving rules they've been taught, AND do what makes sense when these things don't agree. When problem solving is taught as a following-the-rules activity, THAT is what children will default to. But here, subtraction would lead to an incorrect answer!

Looking for words that "tell us what to do" just doesn't always work. Eventually these "key words" become a hindrance to effective problem solving and do nothing for establishing a conceptual framework of "how numbers work".

Important Terms and Phrases

Throughout this book certain terms and phrases will pop up quite often. Some important ones are defined below. Reading through each of them will help to clarify certain key points as you go through the rest of the book.

- **Learning standards** are a set of guidelines for what students should know, understand, and be able to do at each grade level. This is a major shift from most former sets of state learning standards which were generally just lists of topics teachers needed to cover. Now students must demonstrate an understanding of each concept. In this book each big idea is listed and "translated" into "real, every day" language.

- The **vocabulary and terminology** specific to each big idea are defined and explained. Different math text series often use variations of the same term or idea. Wherever possible, we have included known variations to help you understand the terms that may be included in children's assignments.

- The **models** used to represent each big idea are explained and illustrated. Like the vocabulary terms, models and representations often have different names in different math programs. We have included the more popular names of each model wherever possible. We have also included a picture, diagram or example for how each model is used. The illustration will help you determine which model you may be seeing in children's assignments, even if they are called something else.

  Students are exposed to the use of models for problem solving and understanding complex math concepts beginning in Kindergarten. They are taught how, and encouraged, to use models to represent math problems before solving them. While this modeling may seem like an "extra thing to do", research has shown that these models actually create "mental scaffolding" allowing students to easily concentrate on and attach new learning to things they already know. Models are introduced early, and reappear throughout each grade level's topics, with students learning new and more complex ways to use them.

- Students demonstrate **conceptual understanding** when they know which mathematical ideas are important for solving a problem, why these ideas are important, how an idea or procedure can be explained or justified in its use, and how to adapt previous mathematical experiences to new problem solving situations. In other words, they have a strong sense of numbers, how they work, and the skills they bring to each problem solving situation.

- An **algorithm** is a series of "steps" performed in a certain sequence, in order to complete a math calculation. The "standard algorithm" is usually thought of as "the way we learned". It's important to note that today's learning standards still require students to be able to calculate using these algorithms, they simply require students to understand why the algorithms work before being formally introduced to them.

- The term **fluency** applies to things students need to "be fluent" in. "Fluent" in the Standards means "fast and accurate." It is similar to what we mean when we say somebody is fluent in a foreign language: when you're fluent, you flow....no time is needed to mentally rehearse; recall of necessary skills and facts is automatic. In other words, students can perform calculations and solve simple problems quickly and accurately. Required fluencies at each grade level build from student understandings in prior grades. For example, third grade students are required by the standards to "fluently multiply and divide within 100"...this means that in second grade students began the foundational work needed to conceptually understand multiplication.

The information found in this book can, and should, be shared with students. Discovery of the purpose behind what is being done may help some children gain a better understanding when applying this knowledge. Older students will benefit from USING this handbook; they should have one to keep in class, and reference it as they work!

Teachers should keep a copy on their desks as a reference in their daily practice as well as in their planning. This will be useful irrespective of the curriculum (text series) used.

Administrators can use this book as a reference when looking over lesson plans, observing classroom instruction and planning meetings as well as professional development sessions. It also provides a common framework for discussion.

When there are staffing decisions to be made, *Boards of Education* can use this handbook to frame and guide questions for potential candidates. It also provides the necessary outline of today's learning standards to serve as a guide in choosing supplemental curriculum materials.

Again, the importance of a ***common framework*** when discussing mathematics in classrooms, buildings, districts, and students' homes **cannot be stressed enough!**

In the event you are unsure about how to proceed in helping your child, keep our credo in mind:

"We don't REMEMBER how to DO math, we THINK about how to USE math in order to solve problems."

-Christopher Sarlo & Patti J. Dieck

GRADE 4- PATTERNS AND FLUENCY MODELS

Standard Addition Algorithm

Standard Subtraction Algorithm

In/Out Tables

Patterns

Learning standard 4.OA.5 says:

Generate a number or shape pattern that follows a given rule. Identify apparent features of the pattern that were not explicit in the rule itself. For example, given the rule "Add three" and the starting number one, generate terms in the resulting sequence and observe that the terms appear to alternate between odd and even numbers. Explain informally why the numbers will continue to alternate in this way.

What it means:

Children in fourth grade identify and create number and shape patterns. They are able to determine terms in a number pattern, or create new shapes in a shape pattern, by following a given rule. When working with patterns, fourth graders also identify additional pattern-relationships that are separate from the original rule. (For example, when children start at zero or any multiple of 5, and follow the rule "Add five", they observe that each term in the pattern alternates between ending with a 5 and ending with a 0.) When they have identified these additional relationships, children are able to explain why they know the pattern will continue.

The work that fourth graders do with mathematical patterns builds a foundation for the work they will do in later grades. It helps them to understand that numbers behave in predictable ways, and that no matter what "kinds" of numbers they are working with (whole numbers, fractions, decimals, positive/negative integers, etc.) children can apply all of the conventions they are familiar with.

Example:

IN	OUT
9	
11	
14	
16	
n	27

Rule: Add 5

Fill-in the table. Identify the odd and even numbers. Look for a pattern with the IN → OUT that emerges when 5 is added to odd and even numbers:

*9 (odd) + 5 = **14** (even)   **11** (odd) + 5 = **16** (even)   **14** (even) + 5 = **19** (odd)*
***16** (even) + 5 = **21** (odd)   n + 5 = 27 (odd)   **27** (odd) – 5 = **22** (even)*

Explain the odd/even pattern when adding 5.

A child answering this question might reason like this, "When I add 5 to an odd number the sum is even, but when I add 5 to an even number the sum is odd."

They might go on to explain, "I can tell if the sum of 5 and any other number will be odd or even by using this pattern. I don't need to use the table. If 5 is added to any even number the sum will be odd. The opposite will be true any time 5 is added to an odd number."

Finally, he or she would be able to determine that, "n in the table must be an even number, because the sum of n and 5 is an odd number."

Example:

IN	OUT
3	
n	28
10	
12	
m	60

Rule: Multiply by 4

Fill-in the table. Identify the odd and even numbers. Look for a pattern with the IN → OUT that emerges after 4 is multiplied by each odd and even number:

3 *(odd) x 4 =* ***12*** *(even)* ***n*** *(odd) x 4 =* ***28*** *(even)*

10 *(even) x 4 =* ***40*** *(even)* ***12*** *(even) x 4 =* ***48*** *(even)*

m *(odd) x 4 =* ***60*** *(even)* ***60 (even) ÷ 4 = 15 (odd)***

Explain the odd even pattern when multiplying by 4.

A child answering this question might reason like this, "When I multiply both odd and even numbers by 4, the product is always even."

They might go on to explain, "I know that the product of 4 and any other number will be even by using this pattern. I don't need to use the table. If 4 is multiplied by any number the product will be even."

Finally, he or she would be able to determine that, "*n* and *m* in the table can be either odd or even numbers. I can't tell simply by looking at the rule because the product of 4 and any number will be even."

Example:

Identify the pattern shown above, and draw the next two figures.

After studying the pattern, a child might think, "The pattern is 4 sides (quadrilateral/rectangle), 6 sides (hexagon), no sides… 4 sides (quadrilateral/square), 6 sides (hexagon), no sides… 4 sides (quadrilateral)."

"So my first drawing should have 6 sides and my second drawing should have no sides."

Fluency with Addition and Subtraction

Learning standard 4.NBT.4 says:

Fluently add and subtract multi-digit whole numbers using the standard algorithm.

What it means:

Addition Algorithm

Fourth graders should become **fluent** (fast and accurate - *think* fluent speaker of a language) with the standard algorithm for addition. But it doesn't have to mean "from memory". In this case, "fluent" means that students "just know" what to do when faced with two multi-digit numbers that need to be added. They shouldn't need to use a model or place value chart, rather they should be fluent with setting up an addition problem vertically, while properly aligning all of the place values (ones under ones, tens under tens, hundreds under hundreds, etc.) Then they should correctly solve it, using all of the conventions of traditional addition. This includes the concept of regrouping (carrying) digits to new place value columns.

Hundreds	Tens	Ones
3	7	6
+ 2	9	7
1	1	
6	7	3

This model is used in the second grade with the *option* of moving to the standard algorithm. Fourth grade children, however, *should* become fluent with the standard algorithm, as shown in the following example.

Example:

376 + 297 = ?

376
\+ 297
~~1~~ ~~1~~
673

In this example the regrouped digits (numbers that were "carried") are placed across the line dividing the problem and the solution. This may look different from the way most adults learned to add, but it serves an important purpose. When children see the regrouped digit (for example the "1" in the tens column) on the line it is easy for them to see the other digit it is "connected to" (in this case the 3 in the ones column since there were a total of 13 ones.) Placing the digits on the line also makes it less likely that they will be forgotten when children have to add them in to their totals.

Subtraction algorithm

Fourth graders should also become **fluent** (fast and accurate - *think* fluent speaker of a language) with the standard algorithm for subtraction. But it doesn't have to mean "from memory". In this case, "fluent" means that students "just know" what to do when faced with finding the difference between two multi-digit numbers. They shouldn't need to use a model or place value chart, rather they should be fluent with setting a subtraction problem up vertically, making sure they place the greater number on the top of the problem, while properly aligning all of the place values (ones under ones, tens under tens, hundreds under hundreds, etc.) It's important for children to be aware of the relative values of each number in the problem so the numbers are in the correct places in the problem. (When asked, for example, to find the difference between 574 and 791, children need to be aware that 791 is placed into the algorithm first even though it comes second in the written problem.) Then they should correctly solve the problem, using all of the conventions of traditional subtraction. This is includes the concept of regrouping (borrowing) digits to allow subtraction in each place value column.

Hundreds	Tens	Ones
~~6~~ 5	1 2	8
− 3	7	5
2	**5**	**3**

This model is used in the second grade with the *option* of moving to the standard algorithm. Fourth grade children, however, *should* become fluent with the standard algorithm, as shown in the following examples.

Example: 628 - 375 = ?

This work relates directly to children's work with the place value chart, where they first move through each place value column to determine if they *can* subtract.

$$\begin{array}{r} 628 \\ -\ 375 \\ \hline \end{array}$$

If and when it is determined that they "do not have enough", they will need to "borrow/regroup" from the greater place. In this case 2 tens is not enough to subtract 7 tens so one hundred (10 tens) is "borrowed" from the six hundreds (which now becomes 5 hundreds.) The tens place now has 12 tens.

$$\begin{array}{r} {\scriptstyle 5\ 12} \\ \not{6}\not{2}8 \\ -\ 375 \\ \hline \end{array}$$

When children determine that each place *can* be subtracted, they begin subtracting. (Since they have made sure each place is "ready" before doing any subtraction, it doesn't matter if children subtract from right to left or from left to right.)

$$\begin{array}{r} {\scriptstyle 5\ 12} \\ \not{6}\not{2}8 \\ -\ 375 \\ \hline 253 \end{array}$$

**While this may at first look quite different from the way most adults learned to subtract, it is actually very similar. The "borrowing" is done the same way…the difference is that here, ALL of the borrowing is done before ANY of the subtracting. This keeps children focused on one skill at a time, and lessens the chance of errors.*

GRADE 4- PLACE VALUE

By meeting the learning standards in this section, fourth grade children will show that they:

Understand that digits in a place value table increase by 10 times when they shift to the left.

Are able to read and write multi-digit numbers using numerals, words and expanded form.

Can compare two multi-digit numbers.

Can round multi-digit numbers using place value strategies.

Place Value Understanding

Learning standard 4.NBT.1 says:

Recognize that in a multi-digit whole number, a digit in one place represents ten times what it represents in the place to its right. For example, recognize that 700 ÷ 70 = 10 by applying concepts of place value and division.

What it means:

Children in fourth grade use their understanding of place value as the foundation for much of the work they do. The big idea for fourth grade children is that the pattern of the place value table is a constant one. Every time a number is multiplied by 10, it becomes ten times as great as it was, and shifts one place left on the table. A zero fills in the newly created open space in the ones column. When numbers are divided by 10, they shift one space to the right. Children understand this because they are comfortable with the inverse (opposite) relationship between multiplication and division.

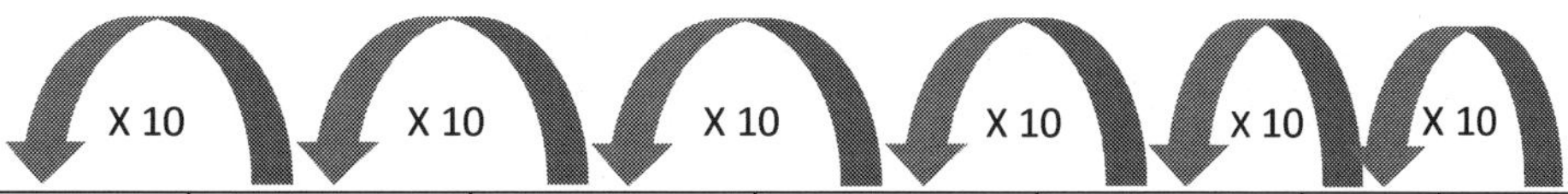

millions	hundred thousands	ten thousands	thousands	hundreds	tens	ones
						3
					3	0
				3	0	0
			3	0	0	0
		3	0	0	0	0
	3	0	0	0	0	0
3	0	0	0	0	0	0

In this chart, three ones (3) becomes three tens (30), then three hundreds (300), three thousands (3,000), three ten-thousands (30,000)…etc, each time it is multiplied by 10. In each case, the three shifts to the left and a zero fills in the ones place.

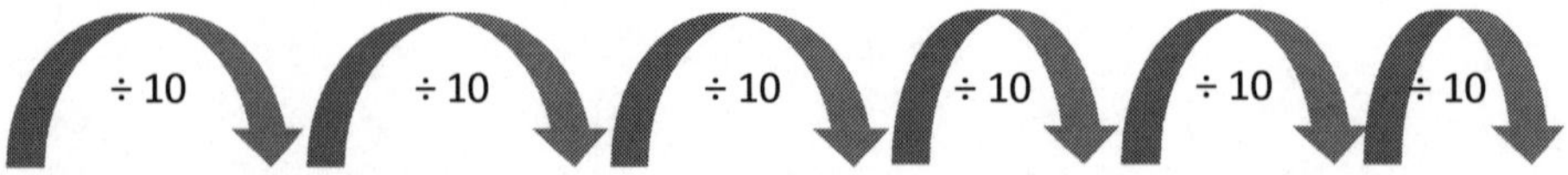

millions	hundred thousands	ten thousands	thousands	hundreds	tens	ones
3	0	0	0	0	0	0
	3	0	0	0	0	0
		3	0	0	0	0
			3	0	0	0
				3	0	0
					3	0
						3

In this chart, three millions (3,000,000) becomes three hundred-thousands (300,000), then three ten-thousands (30,000), three thousands (3,000)…etc. each time it is divided by 10. In each case, the three shifts one place to the right, and a zero is removed.

Comparing Whole Numbers

Learning standard 4.NBT.2 says:

Read and write multi-digit whole numbers using base-ten numerals, number names, and expanded form. Compare two multi-digit numbers based on meanings of the digits in each place, using >, =, and < symbols to record the results of comparisons.

What it means:

In grade 4 children are able to read and write whole numbers that have multiple digits. They can write each number using numerals (often called "standard form"), number names ("word form") and expanded form (where each digit's place value is written out completely.)

To compare whole numbers, children use place value strategies. They record the results of these comparisons by writing number sentences that contain <, >, and = symbols.

The numbers children are asked to compare may be presented in different forms. They may, for example, be asked to compare one number written in standard form to another written in word form. In cases like this, children should be encouraged to rewrite one of the numbers so that it is in the same form as the other one. (Placing each number in a place value chart is a helpful strategy for some children, enabling them to more easily see which of the two numbers is greater.)

Each of the examples that follow shows the numbers being compared within a place value table. This is the simplest way for children to "see" how the digits within two different numbers relate to each other. Eventually, children will be able to visualize this mentally, no longer needing to create the chart. The important thing is for children to rely on place value understanding when determining the relative values of numbers. Some children will move away from the chart more quickly than others…this is OK!

Example:

Use >, <, or = to complete the number sentence (compare):

99,890 ◯ 101,342

(In problems like these, either of the numbers might be presented in word form. In this case a child could simply rewrite it in standard form (as a number) and then put both numbers into a place value chart to compare them.)

A common misconception here is for children see the greater numerals found in 99,890 and believe it is the greater number. When put into a place value chart it becomes easier to "see" that 101,342 occupies more places on the chart. Even though 101,342 is made up of "smaller numerals", children "see" that 99 thousands is actually less than (<) 101 thousands.

millions	hundred thousands	ten thousands	thousands	hundreds	tens	ones
		9	9	8	9	0
	1	0	1	3	4	2

99,890 (<) 101,342

99,890 is less than 101,342

Example:

Use >, <, or = to complete the number sentence (compare):

203,310 ◯ two-hundred three thousand, three hundred one

(Numbers children see in problems like this might be represented in word or expanded form. In either case a child could convert to standard form (as a number) and then put both numbers into a place value chart to compare them.)

Children might rewrite this problem like this:

203,310 ◯ 203,301

When children are first exposed to comparing large whole numbers the importance of using a place value chart to compare numbers is easy to see. It makes a place-by-place comparison more visible. Children will eventually "see" each digit in a number with respect to its place within a number, and will realize how the digits relate to each other. Then it's easy for them to reason that 10 ones (1 ten) is greater than 1 one.

millions	hundred thousands	ten thousands	thousands	hundreds	tens	ones
	2	0	3	3	1	0
	2	0	3	3	0	1

203,310 (>) 203,301

203,310 is greater than 203,301

Example:

Compare using >, <, or = to:

$(2 \times 10{,}000) + (7 \times 100) + (3 \times 10) + (4 \times 1) \quad \bigcirc \quad (9 \times 1{,}000) + (5 \times 100) + (8 \times 10) + (6 \times 1)$

(Any combination of standard form, word form, or expanded form may be represented and/or used by children to help them solve).

Children may also be asked to compare numbers that are in expanded form (as we see in this example.) In this case they can write the numbers in standard form and then put them into a place value chart, or simply fill-in a chart based on each set of parentheses. If they choose the second option it is important they remember to fill-in each place to the right with a zero.

millions	hundred thousands	ten thousands	thousands	hundreds	tens	ones
		2	0	7	3	4
			9	5	8	6

$(2 \times 10{,}000) + (7 \times 100) + (3 \times 10) + (4 \times 1) \quad (>) \quad (9 \times 1{,}000) + (5 \times 100) + (8 \times 10) + (6 \times 1)$

20,734 > 9,586

20,734 is greater than 9,586

Rounding Whole Numbers

Learning standard 4.NBT.3 says:

Use place value understanding to round multi-digit whole numbers to any place.

What it means:

Fourth graders round numbers containing multiple digits to different place values. This means that they will be given a number and asked to round it to a specified place. To do this, children may use whichever strategy works best for them. Similar to when they compared numbers, children may start out using a model, such as a place value chart, and eventually move away from it as they become more proficient at "seeing it" mentally.

The big (and important!) idea here is that children should NOT be taught a series of "rounding steps". Teaching "rounding steps" keeps rounding an isolated skill, not connected to other areas of math. It is much too easy to forget "how to round", when it is not taught from a place of meaning.

The way children in fourth grade are taught rounding is directly related to place value. They should look at the digit in the place they are asked to round to, and then imagine which of those particular units the number would be closest to on a number line. For example, rounding 2,735 to the nearest hundred would require children to first determine that there are 27 hundreds in this number (easily seen in a place value chart.) When picturing 2,735 on a number line, children recognize that it would be between 27 hundreds (2,700) and 28 hundreds (2,800). Finally, children simply decide which group of hundreds 2,735 is closer to. In this case, it is closer to 27 hundreds. So 2,735 rounded to the nearest hundred is 2,700.

Eventually, children will be able to visualize this mentally, no longer needing to create the chart or number line. The important thing is for children to rely on *place value understanding* when rounding numbers. Some children will move away from the models more quickly than others…this is OK!

Example:

Name the underlined place. Round to the underlined place.

3<u>4</u>2

A child solving this problem might use a place value chart or a vertical number line.

millions	hundred thousands	ten thousands	thousands	hundreds	tens	ones
				3	4	2

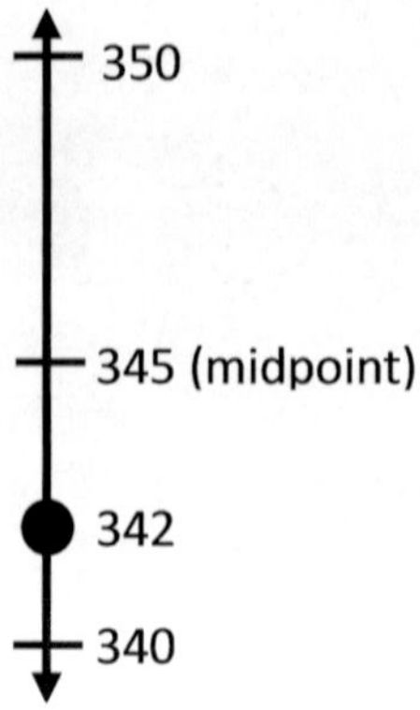

(A vertical number line is often helpful for children to mentally "see" the numbers increasing from bottom to top. This could be replaced with a horizontal line if it is more familiar.)

The 4 is in the tens place (therefore our number line reflects the "tens" that 342 falls between).

345 is the midpoint between 340 (3 hundreds 4 tens) and 350 (3 hundreds 5 tens). 342 is less than the midpoint, therefore it is "closer" on a number line to 340 than 350.

So…

342 rounded to the nearest ten is 340.

Example:

Name the underlined place. Round to the underlined place.

2,687

A child solving this problem might use a place value chart or a vertical number line.

millions	hundred thousands	ten thousands	thousands	hundreds	tens	ones
			2	6	8	7

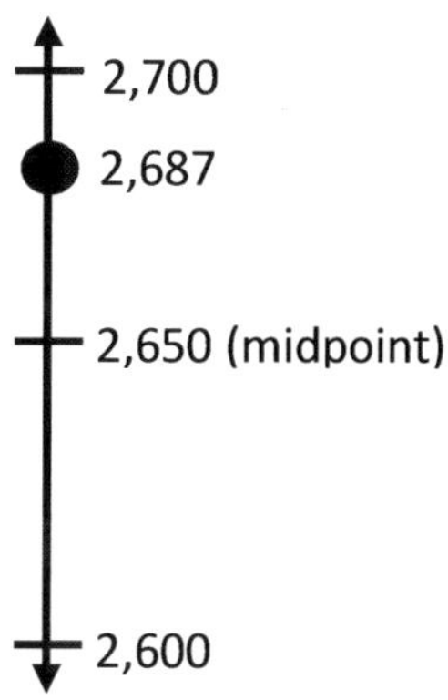

The 6 is in the hundreds place (therefore our number line reflects the "hundreds" that 2,687 falls between.)

2,650 is the midpoint between 2,600 (26 hundreds) and 2,700 (27 hundreds). 2,687 is greater than the midpoint, therefore it is "closer" on a number line to 2,700 than 2,600.

So…

2,687 rounded to the nearest hundred is 2,700.

Example:

Name the underlined place. Round to the underlined place.

35,500

A child solving this problem might use a place value chart or a vertical number line.

millions	hundred thousands	ten thousands	thousands	hundreds	tens	ones
		3	5	5	0	0

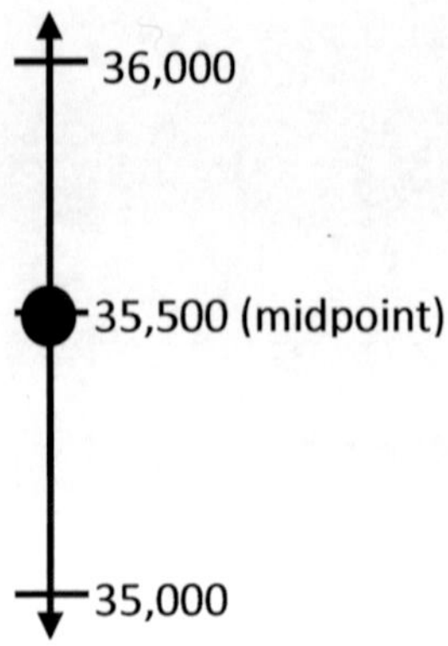

The 5 is in the thousands place (therefore our number line reflects the "thousands" that 35,500 falls between.)

35,500 is the midpoint between 35,000 (35 thousands) and 36,000 (36 thousands). The rule of thumb in cases like this is: when a number is equal to the mid-point it is considered closer to the greater value.

So…

35,500 rounded to the nearest thousand is 36,000.

GRADE 4- MULTIPLICATION & DIVISION

By meeting the learning standards in this section, fourth grade children will show that they:

Are able to interpret multiplication as a means of comparison, and solve comparison word problems.

Are able to find all factor pairs for any whole number between 1 and 100, to determine whether a number is prime or composite.

Multiply a multi-digit number up to four digits by a one-digit number, and multiply two two-digit numbers.

Divide a multi-digit number with up to four digits by a one-digit number, showing the answer as a quotient with or without a remainder.

Understanding Multiplication as Comparison

Learning standard 4.OA.1 says:

Interpret a multiplication equation as a comparison, e.g., interpret 35 = 5 × 7 as a statement that 35 is 5 times as many as 7 and 7 times as many as 5. Represent verbal statements of multiplicative comparisons as multiplication equations.

Learning standard 4.OA.2 says:

Multiply or divide to solve word problems involving multiplicative comparison, e.g., by using drawings and equations with a symbol for the unknown number to represent the problem, distinguishing multiplicative comparison from additive comparison.

What they mean:

When third graders first learned the concept of multiplication, they used a model called a rectangular array (groups of objects organized into a patterns made up of rows and columns, with an equal number of objects in each row.) This helped them understand multiplication as a "fast way" to add multiple groups of the same number.

By the end of third grade children should have memorized all of the multiplication facts up to 10 x 10. Those facts become a tool in fourth grade as children investigate a different way to interpret multiplication. In grade 4 children see multiplication as a means of comparison. Using the phrase "___ times as many as…" for the first time, children learn that multiplication can be used to compare sizes or amounts of things. They learn that 5 x 6 = 30 means the same as "five times as many as six is thirty." Similarly, they see that 30 = 5 x 6 can be interpreted as "thirty is 5 times as many as 6" or "6 times as many as 5".

Fourth graders use this new understanding of multiplication, to write equations that represent word problems. In this way they are learning more about "the language of math"…and how to translate between words and numbers/symbols. Since children understand the relationship between multiplication and division, they apply their new understanding of comparison to both multiplication and division, as shown in the examples that follow.

Example (Multiplication):

Write an equation to solve the following problem.

Chris had to go to 4 meetings last month. Patti went to three times as many meetings as Chris did. How many meetings did Patti go to last month?

To solve this problem a child might think, "Patti went to 3 times as many meetings as the 4 Chris went to, that's the same as "3 x 4". Then he or she writes the following equation: **3 x 4 = ?**

3 x 4 = 12

Patti went to 12 meetings.

Example (Division):

Write an equation to solve the following problem.

Patti went to 12 meetings last month, which was three times as many meetings as Chris went to. How many meetings did Chris go to?

To solve this problem a child might think, "Patti's 12 meetings is 3 times as many as Chris went to, but we don't know how many he went to. That's the same as "3 x ? ". Then he or she writes the following equation: **12 = 3 x ?**

Using what they know about inverse (opposite) operations, children know they can solve this with division:

12 ÷ 3 = ?

12 ÷ 3 = 4

Chris went to 4 meetings.

Prime and Composite Numbers

Learning standard 4.OA.4 says:

Find all factor pairs for a whole number in the range 1-100. Recognize that a whole number is a multiple of each of its factors. Determine whether a given whole number in the range 1-100 is a multiple of a given one-digit number. Determine whether a given whole number in the range 1-100 is prime or composite.

What it means:

Children in fourth grade are most likely familiar with the terms "factors" (two or more numbers that are multiplied) and "product" (the answer when two or more numbers are multiplied). In grade 4 they use their understanding of these vocabulary terms to determine all of the pairs of factors for any number between 1 and 100. Given the number 12, for example, children are able to identify the following factors: 1, 2, 3, 4, 6, and 12. It's important that children remember to include 1 and 12 in this list (or, for other given numbers, 1 and whatever the number is) since these two numbers, when multiplied, make 12. Forgetting to include "1 and the number itself" in factor lists is a very common mistake children make when first learning this concept. With practice, however, it becomes second nature to include them.

In order to create lists of factors for given numbers, children rely heavily on what they know about the multiplication tables. These were likely memorized by the end of grade 3 (up to 10 x 10), but it is not uncommon for fourth graders to still be struggling to memorize a final few. Frequent practice with flash cards or writing out the "tricky tables" once a night is a good idea if children are not completely fluent with these facts.

Fluency with these facts will allow fourth graders to not only list the factors of a given number, but also be able to tell whether a given number between 1 and 100 is a multiple of a specific one-digit number. They will be able to tell, for example, that 36 is a multiple of 6 (but not a multiple of 8.) This is an important skill: Children are forced to expand their thinking about factors and multiplication to include what is traditionally thought of as division. Fostering this connection between multiplication and division is very important for fourth grade children.

Children in fourth grade build on this foundational work with factors and multiples to investigate the new idea of "prime" and "composite" numbers. By comparing lists of factors, children see that some numbers have only 1 and themselves as factors (the only factors of 7, for example, are 1 and 7). These numbers belong to a special group called Prime Numbers. ***Prime numbers are greater than 1 and have exactly two factors.*** Numbers that are NOT prime are called Composite Numbers (*with the exceptions noted below.) ***Composite numbers are greater than 3 and have more than two factors***. (4 is the least composite number....it is the first whole number with more than two factors ...1, 2 and 4.)

There are a few special cases to keep in mind when children learn about prime and composite numbers:

- The number 2 is the ONLY even prime number....simply because every even number after 2 has 2 as a factor.
- 1 is NOT prime or composite....it doesn't fit either category because it has only 1 factor (1 x 1 is the only way to "make 1" by multiplying.)
- 0 is NOT prime or composite...it doesn't fit either category since it is less than 1.

One very common misconception among children in fourth grade is that all odd numbers are automatically prime numbers. While it is true that all prime numbers, except for 2, are odd, this does NOT mean that all odds are prime. Children need repeated exposure to numbers found in the 3, 5, 7 and 9 times tables to truly understand this idea. The more experience children have seeing odd numbers classified as composite, the more comfortable they will become with this idea.

The big ideas here are that children in fourth grade use all of their understanding about factors and multiples to solidify in their minds the relationship between multiplication and division, and to classify numbers as prime or composite. The foundational work they do learning the multiplication tables proves invaluable here.

Example:

List the factors of each number below and then tell if each number is prime or composite.

5	1, 5	**Prime**
9	1, 3, 9	**Composite**
18	1, 2, 3, 6, 9, 18	**Composite**
21	1, 3, 7, 21	**Composite**
23	1, 23	**Prime**
35	1, 5, 7, 35	**Composite**
64	1, 2, 4, 8, 18, 32, 64	**Composite**
71	1, 71	**Prime**
77	1, 7, 11, 77	**Composite**

Whole Number Multiplication

Learning standard 4.NBT.5 says:

Multiply a whole number of up to four digits by a one-digit whole number, and multiply two two-digit numbers, using strategies based on place value and the properties of operations. Illustrate and explain the calculation by using equations, rectangular arrays, and/or area models.

What it means:

The most important idea about multiplication in fourth grade is that even though children will multiply multi-digit numbers, *they are NOT expected to become fluent with the multiplication algorithm until fifth grade.* This means that as fourth graders learn multiplication, the focus should be on them truly understanding **the process**. The methods and strategies that ultimately make the most sense to each individual child are the ones he or she should use. Of course, children will be exposed to the standard algorithm (the way most adults learned), and many will choose to use it. It's extremely important to keep in mind that, just as was the case with addition and subtraction, *not all children will move to using the algorithm at the same time.* This is normal! Children who are NOT pushed too soon to use a single strategy will gain a better understanding of multiplication, and be much less apt to have apprehension about it.

In third grade children gained an understanding of what the concept of multiplication means. They also memorized single-digit multiplication facts. In grade 4 children use these tools to multiply greater numbers, beginning with the multiplication of a two-, three-, or four-digit number by a single digit. There are a number of models and strategies that students might be exposed to in order to accomplish this....hopefully they are exposed to all of these:

- **Area Model** (A model that uses expanded form and what children understand about finding the area of a rectangle to help them visualize and understand multiplication of greater numbers.)
- **Partial Products** (A "bridge" strategy that uses expanded form to help children move from the area model to a written method that is similar to the standard algorithm.)

- **The Standard Algorithm** (The method most adults learned for multiplying greater numbers.)

Fourth grade children multiply two two-digit numbers for the first time. In order to accomplish this, they rely on and apply whichever multiplication strategies they find most helpful. Most children are especially comfortable using the area model for two-digit by two-digit multiplication. It provides them with a very concrete representation of exactly what is happening in this type of problem, and helps them make sense of the work they will do later on with the multiplication algorithm.

Example:

Using an **Area Model** to solve **1,743 x 6**

A child who needs to solve this problem might think "I know that 1,743 x 6 is the same as 6 x 1,743. I can represent it in an area model like this:

	1,000 +	700 +	40 +	3
6	6 x 1,000 6,000	6 x 700 4,200	6 x 40 240	6 x 3 18

After representing the problem like this, the child goes on to think, "Each of the boxes in the area model has one part of the total product. I can add these parts to get the whole thing."

$$\begin{array}{r} 6{,}000 \\ 4{,}200 \\ 240 \\ +\ 18 \\ \hline 10{,}458 \end{array}$$

1,743 x 6 = 10,458

Example:

Using **Partial Products** to solve 1,743 x 6

To solve this problem without a model, a fourth grader might choose to use the partial products strategy. When setting it up, he or she might think, "I can use what I know about the area model to set up a partial products problem. I just have to use expanded form to take apart 1,743. Then I can multiply each part by 6.

$$
\begin{array}{rl}
1{,}743 & = 1000 + 700 + 40 + 3 \\
\times\ 6 & \\
\hline
18 & \rightarrow 6 \times 3 \\
240 & \rightarrow 6 \times 40 \\
4200 & \rightarrow 6 \times 700 \\
+\ 6000 & \rightarrow 6 \times 1000 \\
\hline
10{,}458 &
\end{array}
$$

After multiplying each of the parts, the child thinks, "Since I multiplied each of the parts of 1,743 separately, I need to add the parts together to get the whole product."

1,743 x 6 = 10,458

Example:

<u>Using the **Standard Algorithm** to solve **1,743 x 6**</u>

It is very important to stop for a minute and remember that fourth graders are not required to use the standard algorithm (the way most adults learned to multiply) fluently. This is a fifth grade skill. The goal here is for children to have exposure to the algorithm, and to use what they understand about the area model and partial products strategy to navigate their way through it. Children will work towards fluency with the multiplication algorithm all through fifth grade.

```
 4 21
 1,743
x    6
------
10,458
```

```
 1,743
x    6
-4-2-1-
10,458
```

Notice that in this example, the numbers that were "carried" (the "1" in "18" for example), were placed across the horizontal line separating the problem and the answer. Some children first learned to "carry" this way in second grade when learning to add greater numbers. If this is what children are familiar with, it makes sense to continue it here.

Example:

Using an **Area Model** to solve.

43 x 26

A child who needs to solve this problem might think "I know that 43 and 26 can both be broken into place value parts (expanded form). I can represent this problem in an area model like this:

	40	+ 3
6	6 x 40 240	6 x 3 18
+ 20	20 x 40 800	20 x 3 60

After representing the problem in the model and multiplying the parts, this child might think, "Once I have all of the parts multiplied, I can add them all to find the whole product."

$$\begin{array}{r} 18 \\ 240 \\ 60 \\ +\ 800 \\ \hline \overset{1}{1{,}118} \end{array}$$

43 x 26 = 1,118

Whole Number Division

Learning standard 4.NBT.6 says:

Find whole-number quotients and remainders with up to four-digit dividends and one-digit divisors, using strategies based on place value, the properties of operations, and/or the relationship between multiplication and division. Illustrate and explain the calculation by using equations, rectangular arrays, and/or area models.

What it means:

The most important idea about division in fourth grade is that even though children will divide up to a four-digit number by a single digit, *they are NOT expected to become fluent with the division algorithm until sixth grade.* This means that as fourth graders learn division, the focus should be on them truly understanding the process, because it is laying an important foundation. The methods and strategies that ultimately make the most sense to each individual child are the ones they should use. Children will be exposed to the standard algorithm (the way most adults learned), but it will likely remain a very abstract idea, and most will choose not to use it yet. It's extremely important to keep in mind that, just as was the case with addition and subtraction and multiplication, *not all children will move to using the algorithm at the same time.* This is normal! Children who are NOT pushed too soon to use a single strategy will gain a better understanding of division, and will have more success with the algorithm once they move to using it.

In third grade children gained an understanding of what the concept of division means: breaking a number or quantity into smaller, equal groups. They may also have learned to view division as the opposite (inverse) of multiplication, as well as memorized single-digit division facts. In some third grade classrooms, the focus may have been on memorizing multiplication facts in isolation, leading to children having had little exposure to the division facts. A great way to combat this is to use fact triangle cards, or division flash cards for 10 or 15 minutes each day. Children will quickly make the connection and realize that for every multiplication fact they know by heart they already know the corresponding division fact. Learning to associate division with what they already know about multiplication will build a strong foundation for children as they move through fourth grade math…and beyond.

In grade 4 children use these multiplication and division facts in order to divide two-, three-, or four-digit numbers by a single digit. There are a number of models and strategies that students might be exposed to in order to accomplish this....hopefully they are exposed to all of these:

- **Area Model** (A model that uses what children understand about finding the area of a rectangle to help them visualize and understand multiplication of greater numbers.)
- **Place Value Chart** (A model that is very familiar to children, and when used for division, allows them to see how a multi-digit number should be divided from the greatest to the least place value.)
- **Partial Quotients Method** (A model that bridges children's work with the area model and place value chart to the algorithm.)
- **The Standard Algorithm** (The method most adults learned for multiplying greater numbers.)

The big idea here is that children gain *an understanding* of how division with greater numbers works. They may not be completely comfortable with standard long division yet and this is OK! The important thing is that they can use a place value strategy to complete the division.

The following four examples use the same problem to show how children might progress through the sequence of division strategies. They begin with the familiar place value chart, only moving toward the standard division algorithm as they are ready.

Example:

Using a Place Value Chart and Circles to Divide **142 ÷ 6**

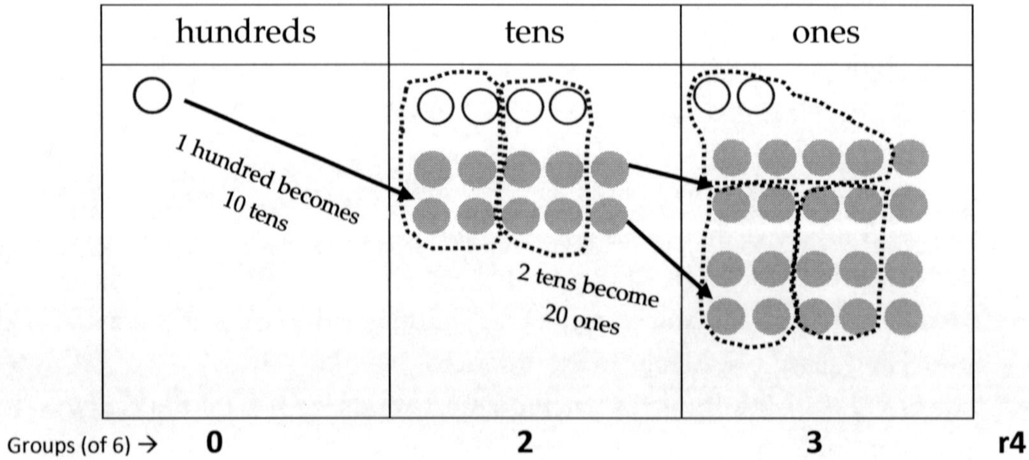

2 tens + 3 ones = 23

142 ÷ 6 = 23 r4

To solve this problem a child first draws a place value chart and places the appropriate number of circles in each section (shown here as the open circles.) Since children are familiar with the idea that division creates equal-size groups, the child begins with the greatest place value and makes groups of 6 (since we're dividing by 6.) A zero is written under the hundreds place since zero groups of 6 were made.

There aren't enough hundreds to create a group of 6, so the hundred is shifted to the tens column, becoming 10 tens (shown here as the closed circles.) Once again, the child looks for groups of 6 circles, and is able to make 2 groups. A two is written under the tens place since two groups of 6 were made.

The two "leftover" tens (that could not be grouped) are shifted to the ones column, becoming 20 ones. In the ones column the child is able to make 3 groups of 6 circles. A three is written under the ones column since three groups were made. Since there are no more columns to divide, the four "leftover" circles become the remainder.

Example:

<u>Using a Place Value Chart and Numbers to Divide **142 ÷ 6**</u>

hundreds	tens	ones
1	**4**	**2**
	14	22
(1 ÷ 6 = 0 groups of 6) (The 1 "leftover" hundred shifts to the tens column.)	6 x 2 = 12 14 – 12 = 2 (14 ÷ 6 = 2 groups of 6) (The 2 "leftover" tens shift to the ones column.)	6 x 3 = 18 22 – 18 = 4 (22 ÷ 6 = 3 groups of 6) (The 4 "leftover" ones become the remainder.)

Groups (of 6) → **0** **2** **3** **r4**

2 tens + 3 ones = 23

142 ÷ 6 = 23 r4

To solve this problem a child first draws a place value chart and places the appropriate digits in each section. Since children are familiar with the idea that division creates equal-size groups, the child begins with the greatest place value and divides it by 6.

There aren't enough hundreds to divide by 6, so a zero is written under the hundreds column and the 1 hundred is shifted to the tens column, becoming 10 tens (turning the existing 4 tens into 14.) Once again, the child divides by 6, making 2 groups.

A two is written under the tens column since two groups of 6 were made. The two "leftover" tens are shifted to the ones column, becoming 20 ones. In the ones column the child divides by 6 and makes 3 groups. A three is written under the ones column. Since there are no more columns to divide, the four "leftover" ones become the remainder.

Example:

Using Partial Quotients to Divide **142 ÷ 6**

When working with this strategy, each place value is divided separately.

A child using this model knows to begin with the greatest place value first (in this case, the hundreds place.) There aren't enough hundreds to divide by 6, so the child records a partial quotient of zero (shown as the bottom number in the answer area.)

Next, the child divides 14 tens by 6. They know that "6 times 2 tens is 12 tens", so 2 tens, or 20, is recorded in as a partial quotient (above the zeros.)

Finally, the child divides 22 ones by 6. Since 6 times 3 ones is 18 ones, 3 is recorded as a partial quotient (above the 20.)

```
      3
     20
    000
   ____
6 | 142
   -000
   ----
    142
   -120
   ----
     22
   - 18
   ----
      4
```

These numbers are placed here as each place value is divided. Because 142 was divided one place value at a time these numbers are parts of the quotient. To finish the problem these numbers need to be added together.

0 + 20 + 3 = 23

*Since all of the place values have been divided, the 4 becomes the

142 ÷ 6 = 23 r4

Example:

Using the Standard Algorithm to Divide **142 ÷ 6**

```
      0 2 3
    ________
6  | 1 4 2
    - 0 0 0   (0 x 6)
    _______
      1 4 2
     -1 2 0   (20 x 6)
    _______
        2 2
     -  1 8   (3 x 6)
    _______
          4
```

The child solving this problem used a similar strategy as the one most adults learned. Instead of dividing each individual digit, and then needing to "bring down" the next digits, the division is done by place value. First the hundreds are divided, then the tens, and finally the ones. The entire place value is subtracted each time, instead of just the single digit.

The big difference here for most adults is the missing "bring down" step. This step isn't needed if the entire number is subtracted at each level. Working this way automatically "brings down" any numbers that still need to be divided.

*See pages 61 and 62 for side-by-side examples of problems solved with and without "bringing down".

GRADE 4- MULTIPLICATION & DIVISION MODELS

Area Model for Multiplication

Partial Products for Multiplication

Multiplication Algorithm

Place Value Chart for Division

Area Model for Division

Partial Quotients

Division Algorithm

Area Model for Multiplication

Area Model- A rectangular model that combines the understanding children have about using multiplication to determine the area of a rectangle with their understanding of expanded form.

To use an area model, children break a multi-digit number into its place values, and place it over the divided rectangle. Once it's set up, children simply multiply the length and width of each section and then add the parts together in order to find the entire product.

A 2-digit number times a 1-digit number

24 x 6

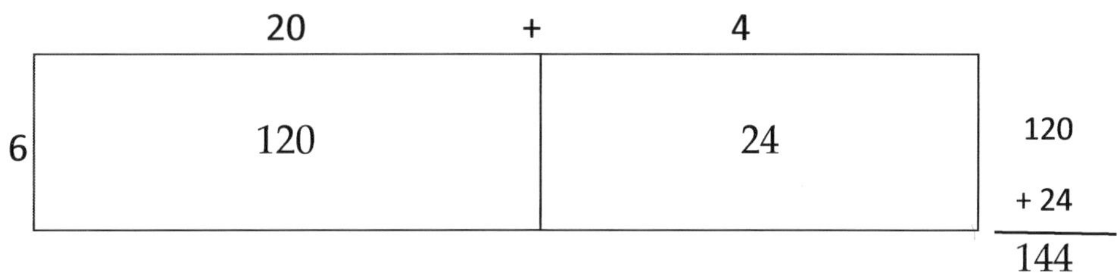

24 x 6 = 144

**In these examples, some of the rectangles are broken into "relatively proportional" size parts (greater numbers are represented by larger sections), while others are divided more evenly. When they are first using this model, children's models may appear more evenly divided. Children should be guided toward creating more proportional size parts, as this gives them another "visual" cue. It makes sense that larger size parts will contain greater partial products. Children can rely on this when determining if their answers are reasonable.*

A 3-digit number times a 1-digit number

324 x 6

	300	+ 20	+ 4
6	1,800	120	24

  1,800
    120
+   24
1,944

324 x 6 = 1,944

A 4-digit number times a 1-digit number

1,324 x 6

	1,000 +	300 +	20 +	4
6	6,000	1,800	120	24

6,000
1,800
120
+ 24
7,944

1,324 x 6 = 7,944

A 2-digit number times a 2-digit number

56 x 72

	50 +	6
2 +	100	12
70	3,500	420

112
+ 3,920
4,032

56 x 72 = 4,032

Partial Products

Partial Products Strategy- With this strategy, children break multi-digit numbers into their place value parts and then multiply each of these parts separately. They add the "partial products" together to determine the whole product. (This strategy serves as a bridge for students, from the area model to the standard algorithm. It is comfortable for children because it is based on place value and looks like the "grown up" way they are getting ready for.)

A 3- digit number times a 1-digit number

1,324 x 6

	1,000 + 300 + 20 + 4	
x	6	
	24	144
	120	
	1,800	7,800
+	6,000	
	7,944	

1,324 x 6 = 7,944

A 2-digit number times a 2-digit number

56 x 72

```
      50 + 6
   x  70 + 2
  ------------
          12   (2 x 6)    }
         100   (2 x 50)   }-- 112
         420   (70 x 6)   }
   +   3,500   (70 x 50)  }-- 3,920
       1
  ------------
       4,032
```

56 x 72 = 4,032

Standard Algorithm for Multiplication

<u>Standard Algorithm-</u> A procedure, or series of steps used for multiplying multi-digit numbers.

Children in grade 4 are not required to be fluent with the use of the standard algorithm. This is a fifth grade standard. They are exposed to it in fourth grade, and are allowed to use it as they feel comfortable. Because it requires more abstract thinking, children are encouraged to rely on whichever multiplication strategies make the most sense to them.

A multi-digit number times a 1-digit number

1,324 x 6

```
   1,3 2 4
 x       6
   1 1 2
 ---------
   7,9 4 4
```

1,324 x 6 = 7,944

*Notice that in this example, the numbers that were "carried" (the "2" in "24" for example), were placed across the horizontal line separating the problem and the answer. Some children first learned to "carry" this way in second grade when learning to add greater numbers. If this is what children are familiar with, it makes sense to continue it here.

A 2-digit number times a 2-digit number

56 x 72

```
      5 6
   x  7 2
     4 1
    -----
    1 1 2
 + 3,9 2 0
    1
 ---------
   4,0 3 2
```

56 x 72 = 4,032

Place Value Chart for Division

Place Value Chart- A model that allows children to separate numbers into their place values and then work with each unit separately.

Place value charts are a familiar model for children; they have been working with these charts since as early as first grade. By fourth grade, children have used this model to assist them with higher level addition and subtraction, rounding and even multiplication by multiples of ten. Their comfort level with this model makes it ideal for introducing division.

Beginning with circles instead of actual numbers allows children to see that as "leftover" units are moved to the right in the chart they must be converted to a group of 10 (Example: 2 tens becomes 20 ones, and 2 hundreds becomes 20 tens when they are moved to the right in the chart.)

Division by a single digit, with no remainder

$252 \div 6$

Since children are dividing by 6 in this problem, they make groups of 6 within each place value. When there aren't enough units to make a full group of 6, the remaining units are shifted one place to the right.

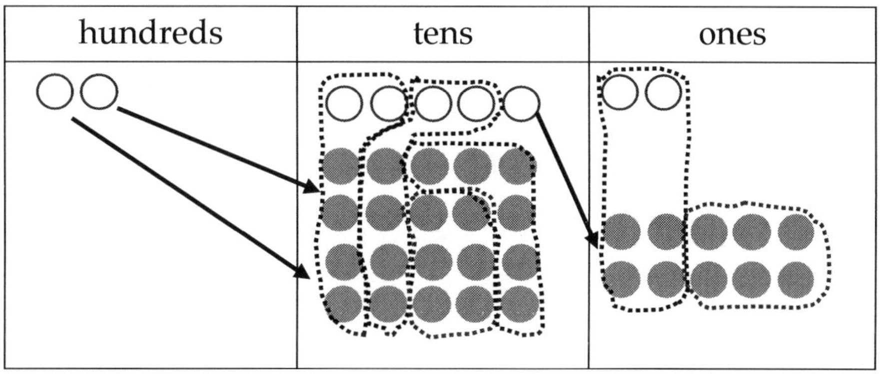

Groups (of 6) → **0** **4** **2**

$\mathbf{252 \div 6 = 42}$

Division by a single-digit number with a remainder

Since children are dividing by 8 in this problem, they make groups of 8 within each place value. When there aren't enough units to make a full group of 8, the remaining units are shifted one place to the right. When the last place value is divided (in this case the "ones place", since we are not working with decimals) the units that remain become the "remainder".

$106 \div 8$

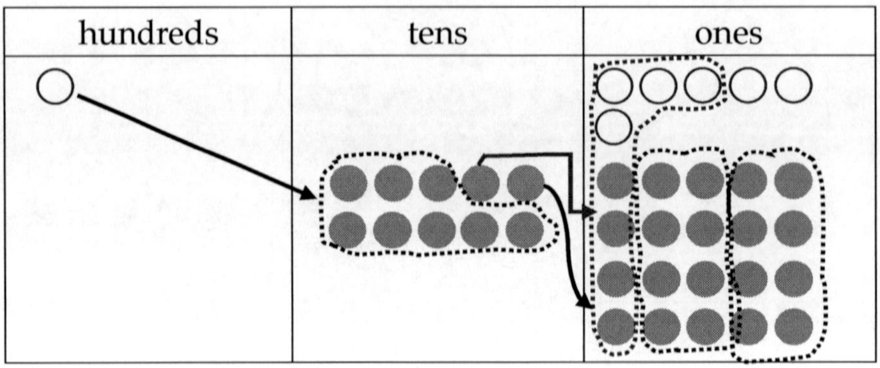

Groups (of 8) → **0** **1** **3** **r2**

$$\mathbf{106 \div 8 = 13\ r2}$$

Division by a single-digit number with no remainder

252 ÷ 6

	hundreds	tens	ones
	2	**5** 25 6 x 4 = 24 25 – 24 = 1 (25 ÷ 6 = 4 groups of 6) (The 1 "leftover" ten shifts to the ones column.)	**2** 12 (12÷ 6 = 2 groups of 6)
	(2 ÷ 6 = 0 groups of 6) (The 2 "leftover" hundreds shift to the tens column.)		
Groups (of 6) →	**0**	**4**	**2**

4 tens + 2 ones = 42

252 ÷ 6 = 42

Division by a single-digit number with a remainder

$257 \div 6$

hundreds	tens	ones
2	**5**	**7**
	25	17
$(2 \div 6 = 0$ groups of 6) (The 2 "leftover" hundreds shift to the tens column.)	$6 \times 4 = 24$ $25 - 24 = 1$ $(25 \div 6 = 4$ groups of 6) (The 1 "leftover" ten shifts to the ones column.)	$6 \times 2 = 12$ $17 - 12 = 5$ $(17 \div 6 = 2$ groups of 6) (The 5 "leftover" ones become the remainder.)

Groups (of 6) → **0** **4** **2** **r 5**

4 tens + 2 ones = 42

257 ÷ 6 = 42 r5

Area Model for Division

Area Model- A rectangular model that combines the understanding children have about using multiplication to determine the area of a rectangle with their understanding of division and multiplication as opposite operations.

To use an area model, children break a multi-digit number into its place values (expanded form), and place them inside the sections of the rectangle. Once it's set up, children simply divide the number inside each section separately and then add the parts together in order to find the entire quotient.

Division by a single-digit number with no remainder

$252 \div 6$

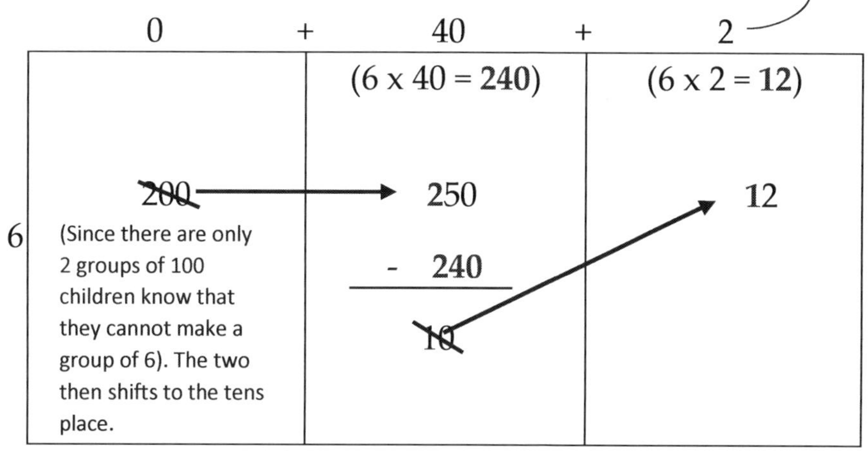

These numbers are placed here as each section is divided. Because 252 was divided one place value at a time these numbers are parts of the quotient. To finish the problem these numbers need to be added together.

$40 + 2 = 42$

$\mathbf{252 \div 6 = 42}$

**If there are some "leftovers" after dividing the "ones", they become the remainder.*

Partial Quotients

<u>Partial Quotient Strategy-</u> With this strategy, children divide multi-digit numbers by each individual place value part separately. They add the "partial quotients" together to determine the whole quotient. (This strategy serves as a bridge for students, from the place value chart and area model to the standard algorithm. It is comfortable for children because it is based on place value and looks like the "grown up" way they have seen before.)

Division by a single-digit number with no remainder

$536 \div 4$

When working with this strategy, each place value is divided separately.

Children know that the 5 in 536 has a value of 500, so "5 hundred" is what gets divided by 4. Children know that "4 times 1 hundred is 4 hundred", so 100 is recorded as a partial quotient.

Next, they divide 13 tens by 4. They know that "4 times 3 tens is 12 tens", so 3 tens, or 30, is recorded in as a partial quotient.

Finally, children divide 16 ones by 4. Since 4 times 4 ones is 16 ones, 16 is recorded as a partial quotient.

```
      4  ┐
     30  ├
    100  ┘
  ┌─────
4 │ 536
   -400
   ────
    136
   -120
   ────
     16
   - 16
   ────
      0
```

These numbers are placed here as each place value is divided. Because 536 was divided one place value at a time these numbers are parts of the quotient. To finish the problem these numbers need to be added together.

$536 \div 4 = 134$

Division by a single-digit number with a remainder

*This problem follows the same procedure as the problem on the previous page.

$478 \div 7$

```
       8    ⎫
            ⎬ 60 + 8 = 68
     0 6 0  ⎭
   _______
7 | 4 7 8
   -4 2 0
   ------
      5 8
   -  5 6
   ------
        2
```

476 ÷ 7 = 68 r2

Since there are no more columns to divide, the "leftover" 2 becomes the remainder.

Standard Algorithm for Division

<u>Standard Algorithm-</u> A procedure, or series of steps used for dividing multi-digit numbers.

Children in grade 4 are not required to be fluent with the use of the standard division algorithm. This is a sixth grade standard. They are exposed to it in fourth grade, and allowed to use it as they feel comfortable. Because it requires much more abstract thinking, and is not a required fluency for two more years, it is OK if children are not yet comfortable or competent with its use. (Remember, the big idea in grade 4 is for children to understand what division means and that, like all operations, division strategies are based on place value.)

Division by a single-digit number with no remainder

$536 \div 4$

```
     134
   ______
 4 | 536
   -4
   ----
     13
    -12
   ----
      16
   -  16
   ----
       0
```

```
        134
      _________
 4    |  536
        -400   (100 x 4)
        -----
         136
        -120   (30 x 4)
        -----
          16
       -  16   (4 x 4)
        -----
           0
```

Division by a single-digit number with a remainder

$478 \div 7$

```
    0 6 8 r2
   _______
7 | 4 7 8
   -4 2
   _______
     5 8
   - 5 6
   _______
       2
```

```
    0 6 8 r2
   _______
7 | 4 7 8
   -4 2 0
   _______
     5 8
   - 5 6
   _______
       2
```

This problem and the one on the previous page are both examples of "the standard algorithm".

On the left is the algorithm the way most adults learned to use it. Each digit was divided separately, beginning with the greatest place value (the hundreds place in this problem). When it was time to divide each digit after that, the digit was "brought down" to be divided, as shown by the arrows.

In the problem on the right, each place value was again divided separately, beginning with the greatest one. Instead of simply subtracting the single digit in each column, and then bringing down the next one, the entire number represented by each digit is subtracted.

GRADE 4 - PROBLEM SOLVING MODELS

By meeting the learning standards in this section, fourth grade children will show that they:

Are able to represent and solve multi-step word problems involving all four operations.

(Use equations (number sentences) with letters in the place of unknown numbers to represent and solve word problems where the numbers in the problems and the solutions are all whole numbers.)

Understand each type of multiplication and division problem.

Recognize and understand the meaning of a remainder in a division word problem.

Models are used for all Multi-Step Word Problems and any of the Four Mathematical Operations.

Multi-Step Word Problems

Learning standard 4.OA.3 says:

Solve multistep word problems posed with whole numbers and having whole-number answers using the four operations, including problems in which remainders must be interpreted. Represent these problems using equations with a letter standing for the unknown quantity. Assess the reasonableness of answers using mental computation and estimation strategies including rounding.

What it means:

The big idea here is that word problems should not be considered a certain "kind" of problem. We should refrain from saying things like, "That's a multiplication and addition problem." Instead, children should be encouraged to determine, and create a model for, the math situation in the problem. This gives them freedom to solve the problem in the way that makes the most sense to them.

Number Bond

Number Bond – A model showing the ***parts-whole*** relationship between 3 or more numbers or quantities. Often used to "break", or decompose, a number into parts in order to make it easier to work with.

Solving One-Step Word Problems

Patti has some number of shells in a bucket. Chris has the same number of shells split into three equal groups. If Chris has 27 shells in each group, how many shells does Patti have in her bucket?

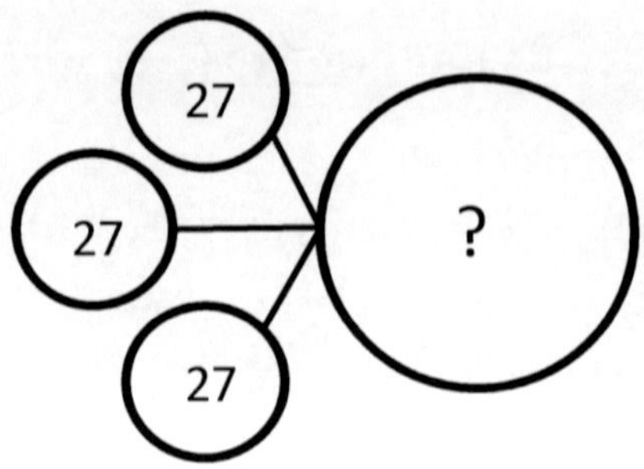

Three equal groups of 27 is 3 x 27.

3 x 27 = *n*

Patti has 81 shells.

The Patriots soccer team is going to watch the Cosmos play. There are 63 students taking vans that each hold 12 people. How many vans will they need?

$$63 \div 12 = v$$

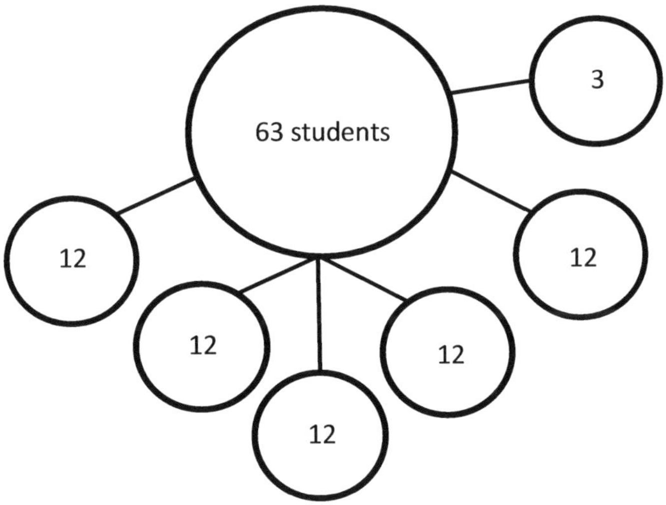

$$63 \div 12 = 5 \text{ r}3$$

They will need 6 vans.

Five vans is not enough because there will be 3 students without a ride. So one more van is needed for a total of 6 vans.

Bar Diagram

(Sometimes also referred to as "Bar Model" or "Tape Diagram")

Bar Diagrams- Bar diagrams help children represent the quantities and situations in math problems, as well as help them decide which operation to use in order to find a solution. After solving each problem, children "place" their answer back into the diagram to determine if it is reasonable.

Solving One-Step Word Problems

Patti has some number of shells in a bucket. Chris has the same number of shells split into three equal groups. If Chris has 27 shells in each group, how many shells does Patti have in her bucket?

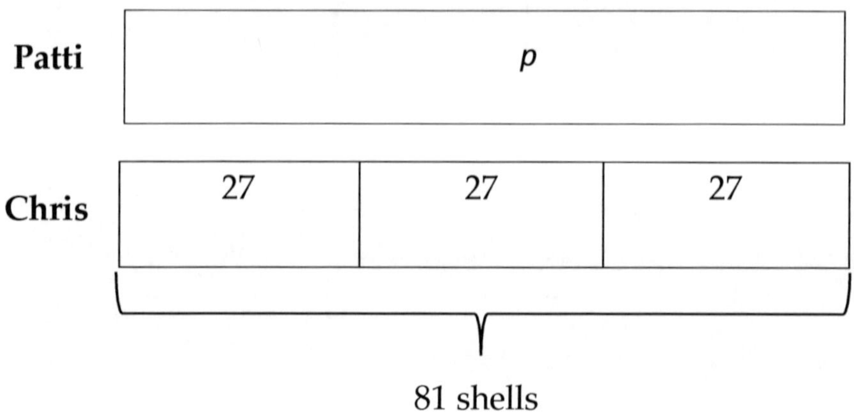

$27 \times 3 = p$

$p = 81$ shells

Patti has 81 shells.

Solving Two-Step Word Problems

Multiplicative Comparison

Gavin and Ian have 49 toy cars. Gavin has six times as many as Ian, how many does each boy have?

49 total toy cars divided into 7 equal groups

49 cars ÷ 7 groups = 7 in each group

Each square is worth 7.

Ian has 7 toy cars.

Gavin has 6 times as many as Ian.

6 x 7 = 42

Gavin has 42 toy cars.

Or

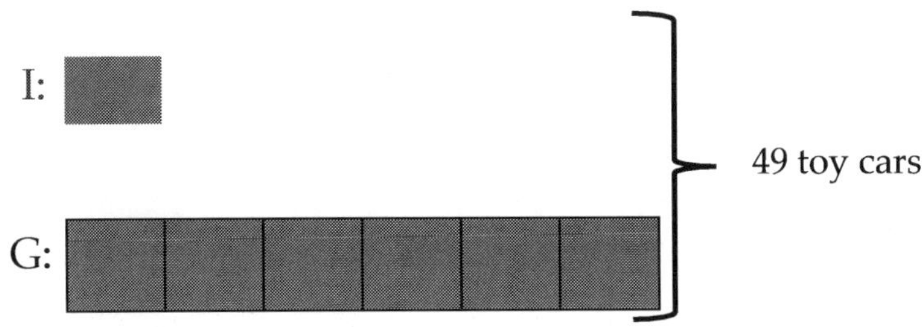

49 total toy cars divided into 7 equal groups

49 cars ÷ 7 groups = 7 in each group

Each square is worth 7.

Ian has 7 toy cars.

Gavin has 6 squares

6 x 7 = 42

Gavin has 42 toy cars.

Ava, Olivia, and Cassie have 40 markers. Ava has three times as many as Cassie and Olivia has twice the number of Ava. How many markers does each girl have?

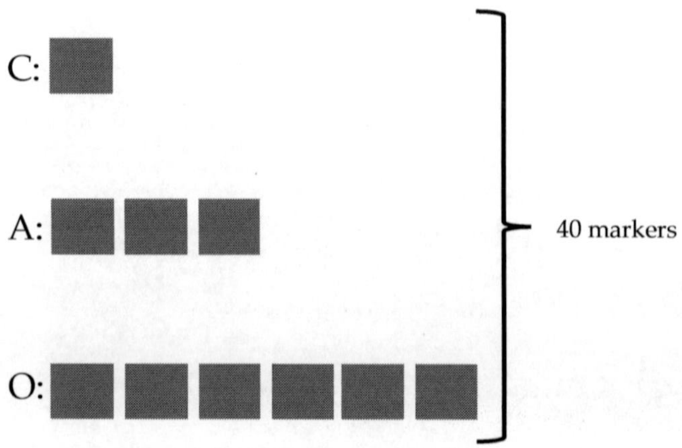

40 total markers divided into 10 equal groups.

40 markers ÷ 10 groups = 4 in each group

Each square has a value of 4.

Cassie has 4 markers.

Ava has 3 times as many as Cassie → **3 x 4 = 12**

Ava has 12 markers.

Olivia has twice the number of Ava → **2 x 12 = 24**

Olivia has 24 markers

Or

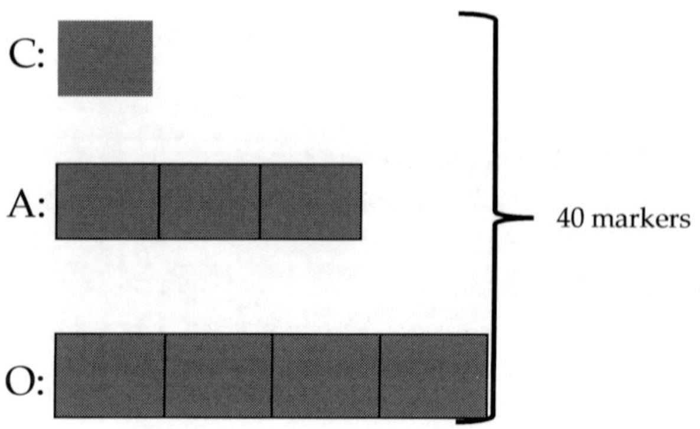

40 total markers divided into 10 equal groups.

40 ÷ 10 = 4

Each square has a value of 4. **Cassie has 4 markers.**

Ava has 3 squares

3 x 4 = 12; Ava has 12 markers.

Olivia has six squares

6 x 4 = 24

Olivia has 24 markers

*Children begin by first determining how many "boxes" each girl has. Since Cassie's total is used to figure out Ava's total Cassie gets 1 box. Ava gets 3 times as many, or 3 boxes. Olivia gets 6 boxes since she has twice as many as Ava. After creating the model children see that 40 is divided among 10 boxes.

Patti has \$ 17.00 to spend at an amusement park, Chris has three times as much, and their friend Janine has \$ 23.00 more than Chris. How much money does Janine have?

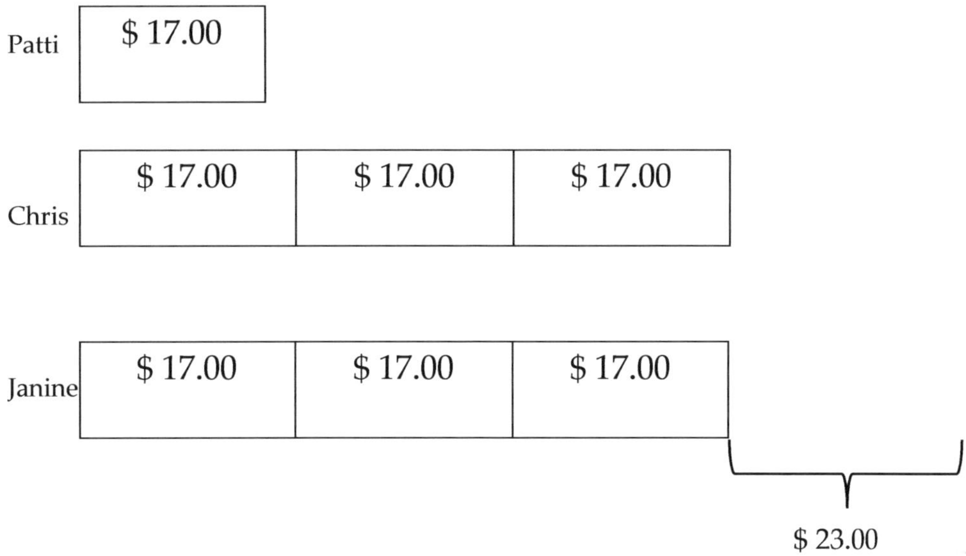

(\$ 17.00 x 3) + \$ 23.00 = j

\$ 51.00 + \$ 23.00 = j

\$ 74.00 = j

Janine has \$74.

GRADE 4- MEASUREMENT

By meeting the learning standards in this section, fourth grade children will show that they:

Know relative sizes of measurement units within one system of units.

(Can tell which units within either the metric or customary system are larger or smaller.)

Can solve measurement word problems.

Are able to apply the area and perimeter formulas for rectangles in real world and mathematical problems.

(Can use a formula to determine and unknown area or perimeter, or find the unknown length of one of the rectangle's sides.)

Converting Measurement Units

Learning standard 4.MD.1 says:

Know relative sizes of measurement units within one system of units including km, m, cm; kg, g; lb, oz.; l, ml; hr, min, sec. Within a single system of measurement, express measurements in a larger unit in terms of a smaller unit. Record measurement equivalents in a two-column table. For example, know that 1 ft is 12 times as long as 1 in. Express the length of a 4 ft snake as 48 in. Generate a conversion table for feet and inches listing the number pairs (1, 12), (2, 24), (3, 36).

What it means:

Children in fourth grade understand that there are different systems of measurement, known as Metric and Customary, to measure length and weight. Within each measurement system, whether for length, weight, or time, fourth graders recognize that larger measurement units can be broken into smaller ones. (For example feet can be broken into inches; yards to feet; meters to centimeters or millimeters). They use this understanding to create tables showing the conversions from larger units to smaller units. There is no set number of conversions each table should contain, the big idea is for children to recognize the pattern they follow to complete each level of the table. This pattern becomes "the rule" of the table, and once the rule is identified, children can use it to determine the number of smaller units in any amount of larger units. They can also list the number pairs they create when filling in the measurement amounts in the table.

It's important to note here that children in grade four only convert larger units to smaller ones. This is because converting smaller units to larger ones (inches to feet, for example) has the potential to result in parts of units, which is beyond the scope of fourth grade work. (15 inches, for example, would result in $1\frac{1}{4}$ feet).

Example:

Create a table to show the rule for converting kilometers to meters.

IN	OUT	
kilometers (km)	**meters (m)**	**number pairs**
1	1000	(1, 1000)
2	*a*	(2, *a*)
3	*b*	(3, *b*)
4	*c*	(4, *c*)
5	*d*	(5, *d*)

A child solving this problem would use the information from the first line of the table to replace the variables in the other lines with the missing numbers. She might reason like this, "If there are 1,000 meters in 1 kilogram, then 2 kilometers would have 2,000 meters, 3 kilometers would have 3,000….etc."

How can you use this table to find the number of meters in 10 kilometers?

To answer this question, a child might think, "I can just double the number of meters in 5 kilometers. Double 5,000 is 10,000 so the answer is 10,000 kilometers."

Or

A child might apply the rule of the table:

# of kilometers x 1,000 = # of meters

IN x 1,000 = **OUT** (Rule: x 1,000)

10 x 1,000 = 10,000 kilometers

Example:

Create a table to show the rule for converting meters to centimeters.

IN	OUT	
meters (m)	**centimeters (cm)**	**number pairs**
1	100	(1, 100)
2	*a*	(2, *a*)
3	*b*	(3, *b*)
4	*c*	(4, *c*)
5	*d*	(5, *d*)

A child solving this problem would use the information from the first line of the table to replace the variables in the other lines with the missing numbers. She might reason like this, "If there are 100 centimeters in 1 meter, then 2 meters would have 200 centimeters, 3 meters would have 300….etc."

How can you use this table to find the number of centimeters in 15 meters?

To answer this question, a child might think, "I can just triple (multiply by 3) the number of centimeters in 5 meters. Three times 500 is 1,500 so the answer is 1,500 centimeters."

Or

A child might apply the rule of the table:

# of meters x 100 = # of centimeters

IN** x 100* = ***OUT (Rule: x 100)

15 x 100 = 1,500 centimeters

Example:

Create a table to show the rule for converting feet to inches.

IN	OUT	
feet (ft)	**inches (in)**	**number pairs**
1	12	(1, 12)
2	a	$(2, a)$
3	b	$(3, b)$
4	c	$(4, c)$
5	d	$(5, d)$

A child solving this problem would use the information from the first line of the table to replace the variables in the other lines with the missing numbers. She might reason like this, "If there are 12 inches in 1 foot, then 2 feet would have 24 inches, 3 feet would have 36….etc."

How can you use this table to find the number of inches in 10 feet?

To answer this question, a child might think, "I can just double the number of inches in 5 feet. Two times 60 is 120 so the answer is 120 inches."

Or

A child might apply the rule of the table:

# of feet x 12 = # of inches

IN x 12 = **OUT** (Rule: x 12)

10 x 12 = 120 inches

Example:

Create a table to show the rule for converting yards to feet.

IN yard(s) (yds)	OUT feet (ft)	number pairs
1	3	(1, 3)
2	*a*	(2, *b*)
3	*b*	(3, *c*)
4	*c*	(4, *d*)
5	*d*	(5, *e*)

A child solving this problem would use the information from the first line of the table to replace the variables in the other lines with the missing numbers. She might reason like this, "If there are 3 feet in 1 yard, then 2 yards would have 6 feet, 3 yards would have 9....etc."

How can you use this table to find the number of feet in 9 yards?

To answer this question, a child might think, "I can just triple (multiply by 3) the number of feet in 3 feet. Three times 9 is 27 so the answer is 27 feet."

Or

A child might apply the rule of the table:

# of yards x 3 = # of feet

IN x 3 = **OUT** (Rule: x 3)

9 x 3 = 27 feet

Example:

Create a table to show the rule for converting pounds to ounces.

IN	**OUT**	
pounds (lbs)	**ounces (oz)**	**number pairs**
1	16	(1, 16)
2	*a*	(2, *a*)
3	*b*	(3, *b*)
4	*c*	(4, *c*)
5	*d*	(5, *d*)

A child solving this problem would use the information from the first line of the table to replace the variables in the other lines with the missing numbers. She might reason like this, "If there are 16 ounces in 1 pound, then 2 pounds would have 32 ounces, 3 pounds would have 48….etc."

How can you use this table to find the number of ounces in 13 pounds?

To answer this question a child might think, "I can double the number of ounces in 5 pounds and add the number of ounces in 3 pounds."

Or

A child might apply the rule of the table:

# of pounds x 16 = # of ounces

IN x 16 = **OUT** (Rule: x 16)

13 x 16 = 208 ounces

Example:

Create a table to show the rule for converting minutes to seconds.

IN minutes (mins)	**OUT** seconds (secs)	number pairs
1	60	(1,60)
2	*a*	(2, *a*)
3	*b*	(3, *b*)
4	*c*	(4, *c*)
5	*d*	(5, *d*)

A child solving this problem would use the information from the first line of the table to replace the variables in the other lines with the missing numbers. She might reason like this, "If there are 60 seconds in 1 minute, then 2 minutes would have 120 seconds, 3 minutes would have 180….etc."

How can you use this table to find the number of seconds in 8 minutes?

To answer this question a child might think, "I can just add the number of seconds in 5 minutes with the number of seconds in 3 minutes."

300 + 180 = 480 seconds

Or

A child might apply the rule of the table:

# of minutes x 60 = # of seconds

IN x 60 = **OUT** (Rule: x 60)

8 x 60 = 480 seconds

Measurement Word Problems

Learning standard 4.MD.2 says:

Use the four operations to solve word problems involving distances, intervals of time, liquid volumes, masses of objects, and money, including problems involving simple fractions or decimals, and problems that require expressing measurements given in a larger unit in terms of a smaller unit. Represent measurement quantities using diagrams such as number line diagrams that feature a measurement scale.

What it means

Children in fourth grade solve measurement word problems. Although they've solved problems with measurement in earlier grades, in grade 4 the problems call for changing the way one or more measurement is expressed. After reading each problem, children determine what to do in order to have only one measurement unit represented in the problem. Once they have expressed each measurement in the same unit, they go on to solve the problem, using that unit in their solution. It is important to note here that children should leave their answers in the unit called for in the problem. They are not expected to convert solutions to larger units. (For example, a solution of "22 inches" should not be converted to "1 foot 10 inches".)

Example:

The power cord for Matthew's laptop is 45 inches long. The power strip it is connected to is 2 feet long. Matthew's computer desk is five feet away from the outlet. Will the power cord and power strip reach the outlet when the computer is on his desk?

A child solving this problem might think, "There are feet and inches in this problem. I have to change the feet into inches so I can solve this problem."

1 foot = 12 inches so 2 feet = 24 inches.

45 + 24 = 69 inches

"Matthew's desk is five feet away from the outlet. 5 x 12 is 60 inches, so that's how long the cord needs to be. The cord will be 69 inches. So yes, the cord and strip will reach.

Area and Perimeter

Learning standard 4.MD.3 says:

Apply the area and perimeter formulas for rectangles in real world and mathematical problems. For example, find the width of a rectangular room given the area of the flooring and the length, by viewing the area formula as a multiplication equation with an unknown factor.

What it means:

Fourth graders have worked with the concepts of area and perimeter in earlier grades. They build on these ideas in fourth grade, eventually using formulas to solve area and perimeter problems. Fourth grade work with formulas builds on the foundation children built in third grade when they discovered that:

- To find perimeter of any polygon they can add the total of the sides **(P = sum of the sides)**. For rectangles they can double the length and width and add them together **(P = 2 x L + 2 x W).**

- To find the area of a rectangle, they multiply the length by the width **(A = L x W).**

In fourth grade these ideas about area and perimeter are formalized. They are written and referred to as **formulas.**

The big idea here is for children to understand that a formula will always work. Once they have this understanding, children are able to use the area formula to determine the area of a rectangle, as well as find a missing length or width when they already know the area. When they know the perimeter, they can use the formula to find the length of an unknown side.

Example: (Finding the perimeter.)

Vincent is building a rectangular sandbox for his children. How many feet of wood does he need to build the sides of the figure shown below?

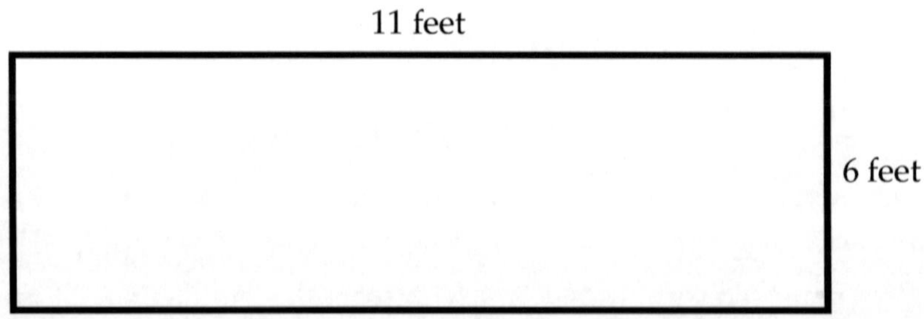

Write an equation and solve.

A child solving this problem might think. "I need to find the perimeter. I can use the formula **P = sum of the sides.**

$$11 + 11 + 6 + 6 = n$$

$$n = 34$$

Another child solving this problem might use the formula **P = 2W + 2L**

$$(2 \times 11) + (2 \times 6) = n$$

$$34 = n$$

Vincent needs 34 feet of wood.

Example: (Finding the perimeter.)

Daniel and Jared are building a patio with the measurements seen below. Before they pour the cement they need to place a wood frame around the area. How many feet of wood will they need? Write an equation and solve.

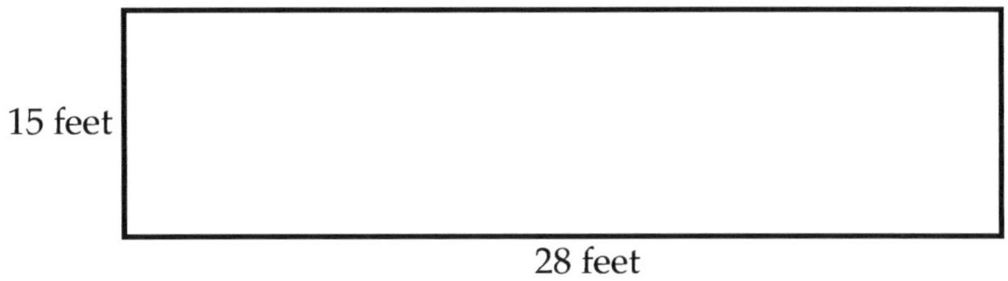

P = sum of the sides

$15 + 15 + 28 + 28 = n$

86 feet of wood fence

Or

P = 2W + 2 L

$(15 \times 2) + (28 \times 2) = n$

$86 = n$

Daniel and Jared will need 86 feet of wood fence.

Example: (Finding the area.)

Daniel and Jared want to cover the entire patio in 1-foot square tiles. How many tiles will they need? Write an equation and solve.

$A = L \times W$

$n = 15 \times 28$

$n = 420$

Daniel and Jared will need 420 tiles.

Example: (Finding an unknown side length.)

Janine's kitchen has an area of 135 square feet. She is covering the floor with 1ft x 1ft square tiles. How many tiles will she need for the length if the floor is 9 tiles wide?

Write a multiplication equation and solve for the missing side length.

$$A = L \times W$$

$$135 \text{ square feet} = \boldsymbol{m} \times 9$$

To solve this problem a child thinks, "I know the area and the width, so I need to find the length. That means I have an unknown factor when I write my equation. I know I can use division to solve missing factor multiplication problems."

$$135 \div 9 = \boldsymbol{m}$$

$$15 = \boldsymbol{m}$$

Janine will need 15 tiles for the length of her kitchen.

* Some children may still have difficulty visualizing a problem like this one. These children should be encouraged to draw and label a rectangle representing the problem. In this case, the rectangle would represent the kitchen. Once children write in the measurements given in the problem and label the length with a question mark, they will much more readily "see" what they should do to solve the problem.

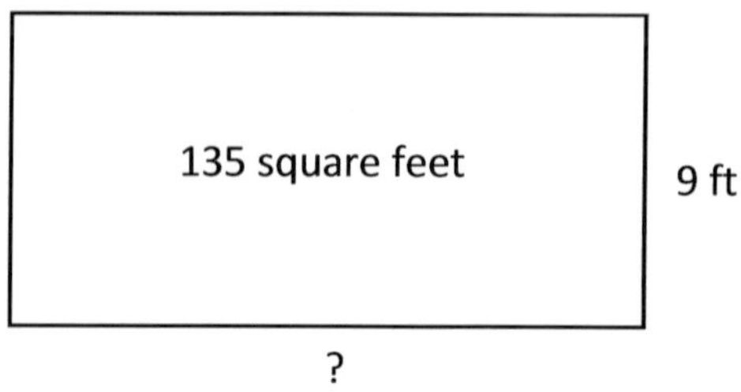

GRADE 4- GEOMETRY AND GEOMETRIC MEASUREMENT

By meeting the standards in this section, fourth grade children will show that they:

Can draw points, lines (parallel and perpendicular), line segments, rays, and angles (right, acute, obtuse).

Are able to classify two-dimensional figures based on the presence or absence of parallel or perpendicular lines, or the presence or absence of angles of a specified size.

Can recognize and/or draw a line of symmetry for a two-dimensional figure.

Can measure angles in whole-number degrees using a protractor.

Understand that angles sharing a side can be added to form a larger angle.

Points, Angles and Lines

Standard 4.G.1 says:

Draw points, lines, line segments, rays, angles (right, acute, obtuse), and perpendicular and parallel lines. Identify these in two-dimensional figures.

Standard 4.G.2 says:

Classify two-dimensional figures based on the presence or absence of parallel or perpendicular lines, or the presence or absence of angles of a specified size. Recognize right triangles as a category, and identify right triangles.

What they mean:

Fourth graders define and draw geometric figures including points, lines, line segments, rays, and angles. They classify different types of angles: right, acute and obtuse, as well as different types of lines: parallel and perpendicular. In addition to classifying these lines and angles, children in fourth grade identify them in two-dimensional figures.

These foundational geometry skills are what children build on when they classify two-dimensional figures based on whether or not they contain certain attributes. They look for pairs of parallel or perpendicular lines, as well as whether or not shapes have different types of angles. Children use this information to reason, for example, about why one four sided figure is considered a square, but another is a rhombus or rectangle. This work is an extension of the geometry work children have been doing since Kindergarten, and it lays an important foundation for grade five. Children have learned previously, for example, that a rectangle has *two sets of equal sides and four "square corners"*. In fourth grade they extend this understanding to mean *two sets of parallel sides and four right angles*.

In addition to classifying four-sided figures, children also identify right triangles (triangles that contain one 90-degree angle), and explain why they belong to this special category.

Geometry Models and Definitions

Point

Point- An exact location. It has no size, only location.

*Note:
The points shown here have been purposefully exaggerated. They will not (and do not have to) always appear very large.

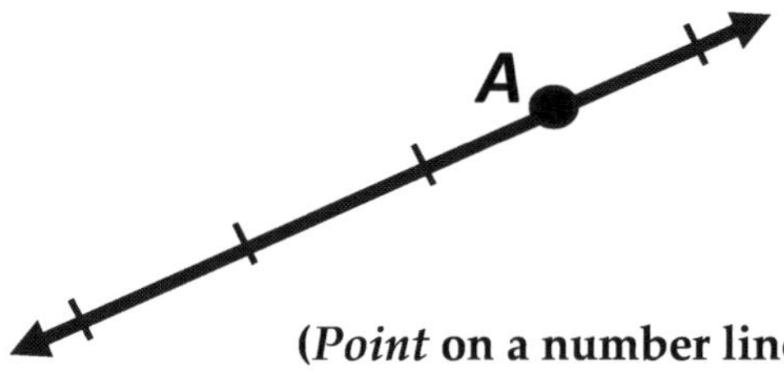

(*Point* on a number line)

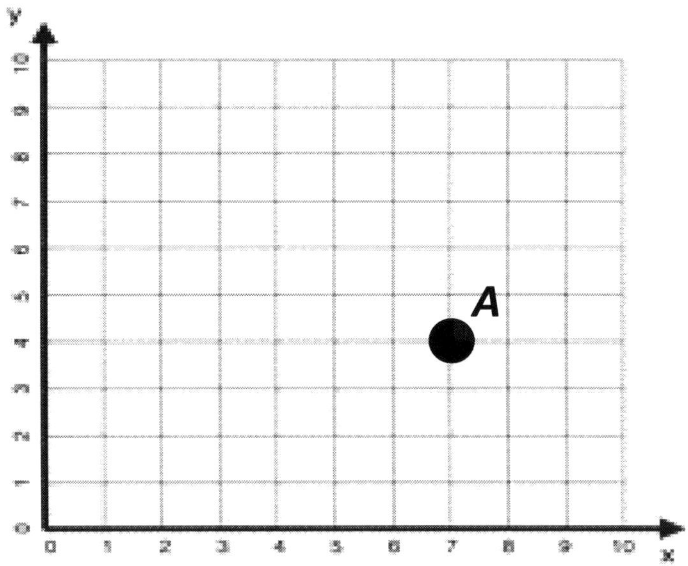

***Point* on a graph/grid**

Lines

<u>Line</u> - a straight path that extends without end (infinitely) in opposite directions. (Drawn with an arrow on each end.)

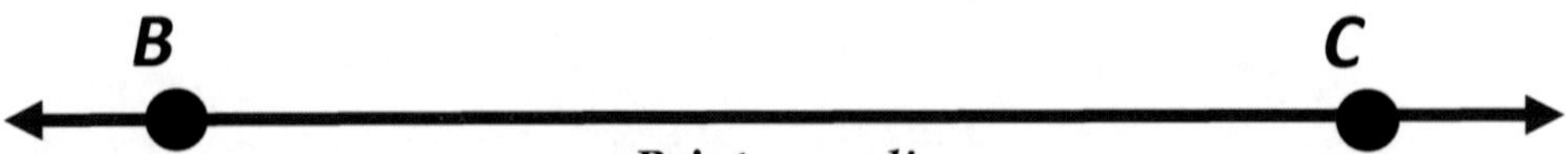

Points on a *line*

$\overleftrightarrow{BC}$ is read left to right **as *"line BC"***

<u>Line Segment</u>- a straight path that connects two points on a line, but does not continue infinitely. (Drawn without arrows.)

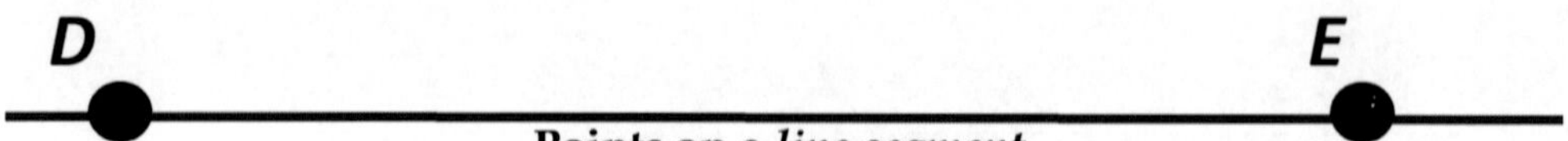

Points on a *line segment*

$\overline{DE}$ is read left to right as ***"line segment* DE"**

<u>Ray</u>- a straight path that extends infinitely in only one direction from a fixed point. (Drawn with only one arrow.)

Points on a *ray*

$\overrightarrow{FG}$ is read left to right as ***"ray* FG"**

Parallel Lines- lines on a plane (a flat two-dimensional surface) that never meet. They are always the same distance apart.

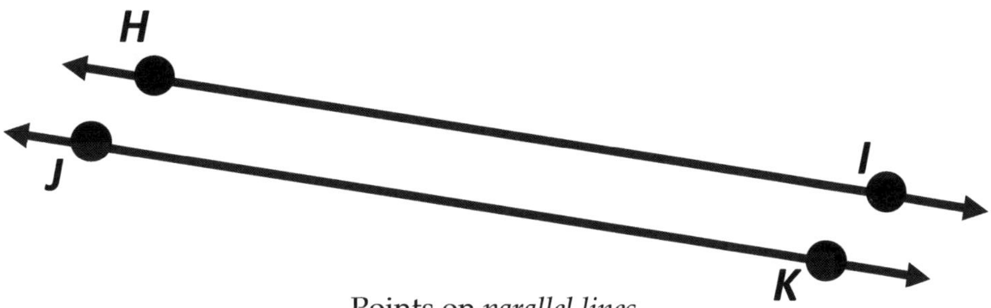

Points on *parallel lines*

$\overleftrightarrow{HI} \parallel \overleftrightarrow{JK}$ is read left to right as ***"line* HI *is parallel to line* JK"**

Perpendicular lines- lines on a plane that intersect (meet or cross) to form a 90-degree angle (right angle).

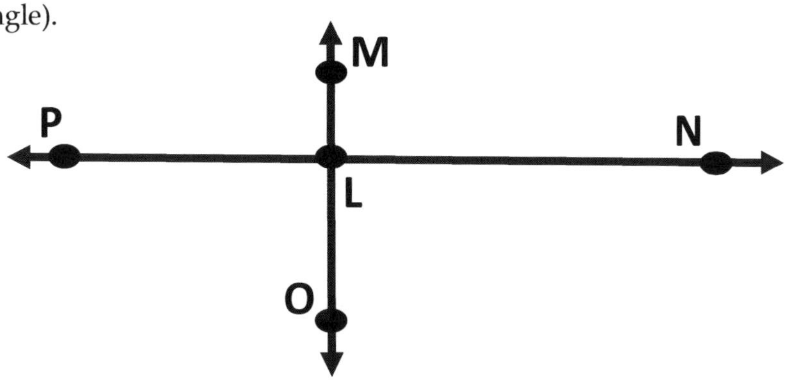

Points on *perpendicular lines*

$\overleftrightarrow{MO} \perp \overleftrightarrow{PN}$ is read left to right as ***"line* MO *is perpendicular to line* PN"**

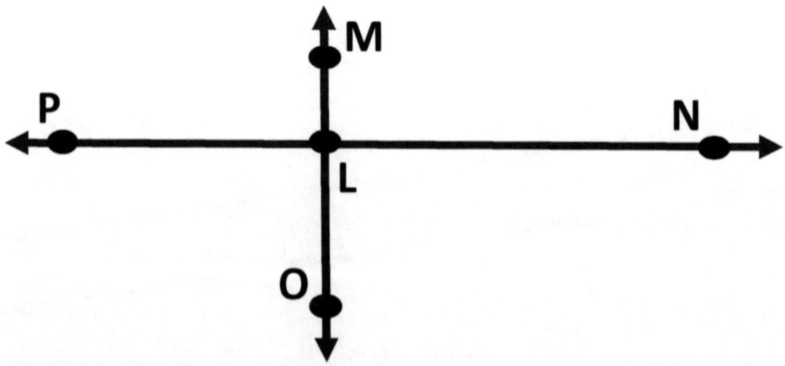

The diagram above can be described in numerous ways:

1) $\overleftrightarrow{MO} \perp \overleftrightarrow{NP}$
   Line **MO** *is perpendicular to line* **NP.**

2) $\overrightarrow{LM} \perp \overrightarrow{LN}, \overrightarrow{LP}$, and $\overleftrightarrow{PN}$
   Ray **LM** *is perpendicular to ray* **LN,** *ray* **LP,** and *line* **PN.**

3) $\overrightarrow{LO} \perp \overrightarrow{LP}, \overrightarrow{LN}$, and $\overleftrightarrow{PN}$
   Ray **LO** *is perpendicular to ray* **LP,** *ray* **LN,** and *line* **PN.**

4) $\overrightarrow{LP} \perp \overrightarrow{LM}, \overrightarrow{LO}$, and $\overleftrightarrow{MO}$
   Ray **LP** *is perpendicular to ray* **LM,** *ray* **LO,** and *line* **MO.**

5) $\overrightarrow{LN} \perp \overrightarrow{LM}, \overrightarrow{LO}$, and $\overleftrightarrow{MO}$

   Ray **LN** *is perpendicular to ray* **LM,** *ray* **LO,** and *line* **MO**

Definitions of Two-Dimensional Shapes

(Children in fourth grade understand that shapes are classified based on their sides and angles. The size, orientation and color of a shape do not affect the shape's classification.)

**Important to note that all geometric shapes MUST be closed (sides must "connect" – no open spaces).*

Triangle – A two-dimensional shape with three straight sides of equal or different lengths, and three angles. ONE angle may be a right angle. When one angle is a right angle, the triangle is classified as a "right triangle". (A triangle may be any orientation, size, or color.)

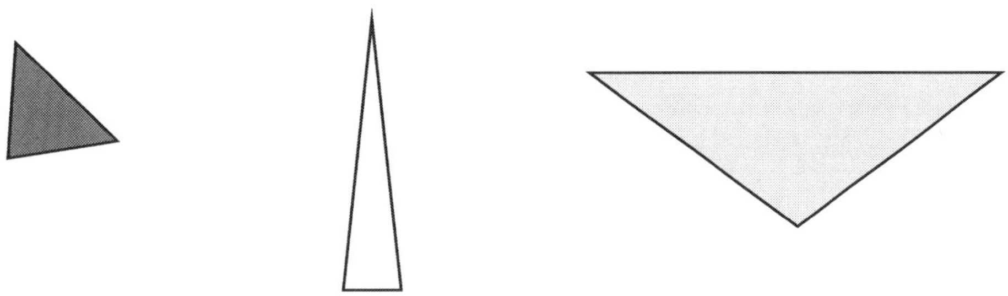

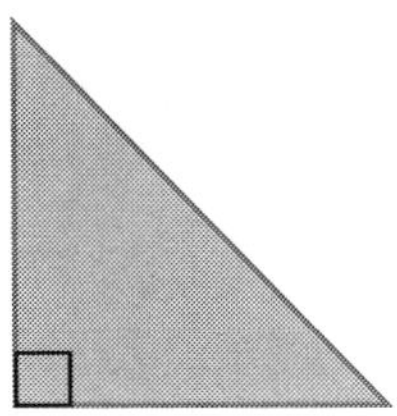

Right triangle

*Quadrilaterals**

*Defined as having four sides and four angles. The following shapes are part of the more general category of quadrilaterals.

Categories of Quadrilaterals

Rectangle – A two-dimensional shape with four straight sides and four right angles. Opposite sides are congruent (equal length) and parallel.

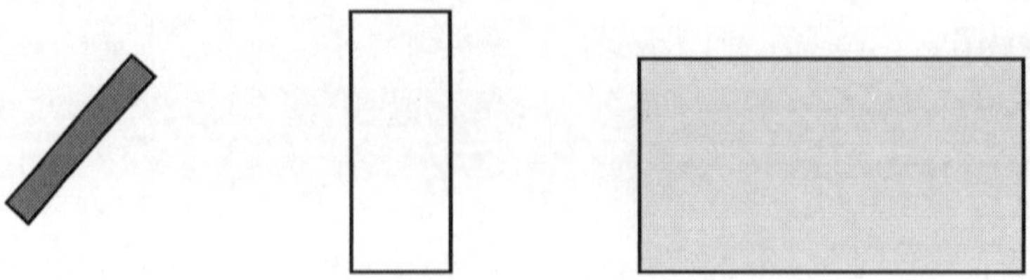

Square – A two-dimensional shape with four straight, congruent sides and four right angles.

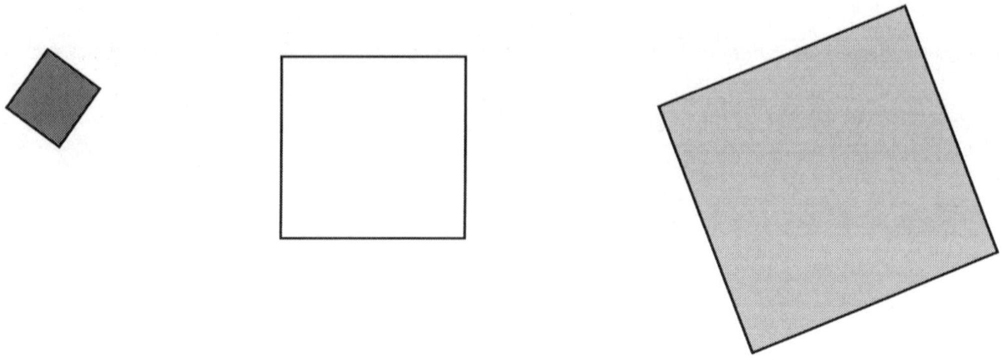

Rhombus – A two-dimensional shape with four straight, congruent (equal length) sides and four angles. Angles can all be right (90 degrees) angles, or opposite angles can be equivalent acute and equivalent obtuse.

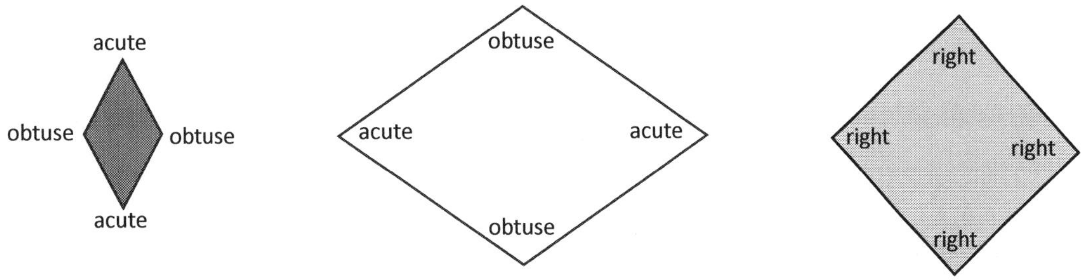

Trapezoid – A two-dimensional shape with four straight sides and four angles. ONE set of opposite sides must be parallel (can have both sets parallel). MAY have ONE or TWO right angle(s).

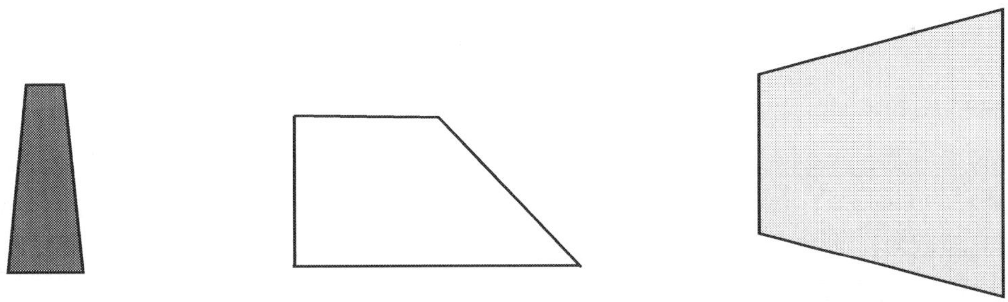

Lines of Symmetry

Learning standard 4.G.3 says:

Recognize a line of symmetry for a two-dimensional figure as a line across the figure such that the figure can be folded along the line into matching parts. Identify line-symmetric figures and draw lines of symmetry.

What it means:

Fourth graders understand that when a figure contains a *line of symmetry* it means that if the figure were folded directly on that line, both sides of the figure would match perfectly. Figures that contain a line of symmetry are also sometimes called *line symmetric* figures. Children in fourth grade also understand that some figures contain more than one line of symmetry, while other figures do not contain any.

When working with symmetry, fourth grade children determine whether or not two-dimensional figures contain lines of symmetry. They also draw lines of symmetry into line symmetric figures, and draw the missing half of a figure when they are given one half and the line of symmetry.

While the concept of symmetry isn't a complex one, at this age some children have difficulty visualizing it in different shapes. They might have trouble, for example, "seeing" that a square has more lines of symmetry than a rectangle. It is often very helpful for children to first explore symmetry by actually folding cut out shapes. Once they fold a square four different ways, and then try to do the same thing with a rectangle they are able to understand that the rectangle's corners will not match perfectly when it is folded on the diagonals. A square, they will see, has four lines of symmetry, but the rectangle will only have two. Similarly, children often think no triangle could have a line of symmetry, but folding a variety of triangles helps them see this is not true.

Understanding the concept of symmetry will lay a useful foundation for children as they move on to later grades and more complex work with geometry and angle measurement.

Example:

How many lines of symmetry does each figure below have? Draw them.

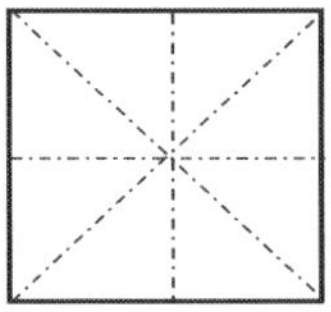

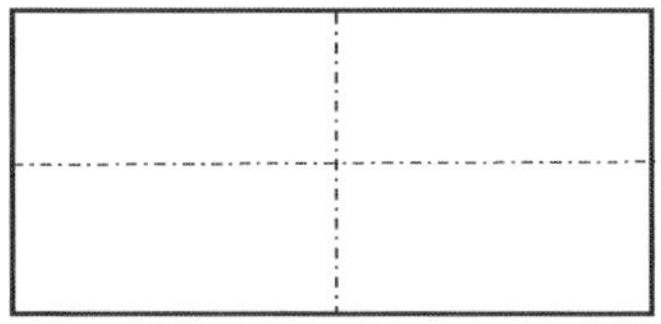

A child answering this question might think, "Since the sides on a square are equal, it can be folded in half four different ways. So a square has four lines of symmetry. But the rectangle only has two lines of symmetry because the corners won't match perfectly if it gets folded diagonally."

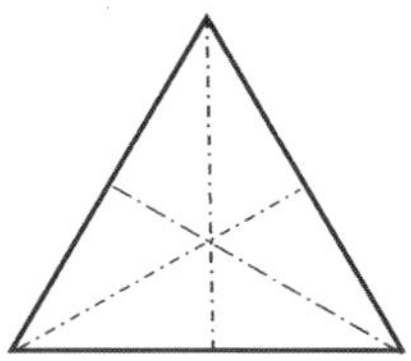

"This triangle has equal sides, so it can be folded in half on each side. That means it has three lines of symmetry."

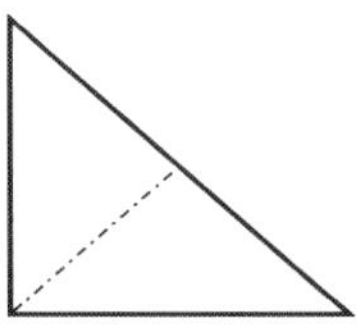

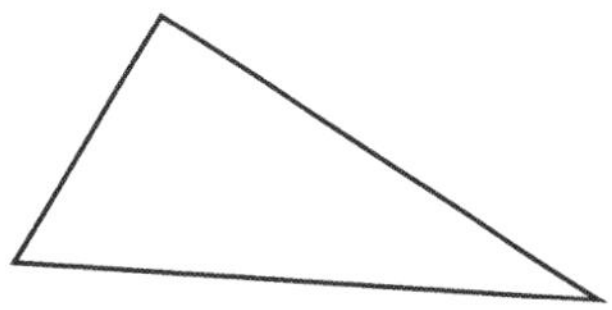

"Since the triangle on the left has two equal sides there is one way it could be folded to make the sides match perfectly. That means it has one line of symmetry. But the triangle on the right has no lines of symmetry. There is no way it could be folded so that two sides match up perfectly."

Understanding Angles

Learning standard 4.MD.5 says:

Recognize angles as geometric shapes that are formed wherever two rays share a common endpoint, and understand concepts of angle measurement:

An angle is measured with reference to a circle with its center at the common endpoint of the rays, by considering the fraction of the circular arc between the points where the two rays intersect the circle. An angle that turns through 1/360 of a circle is called a "one-degree angle," and can be used to measure angles.

An angle that turns through n one-degree angles is said to have an angle measure of n degrees.

What it means:

Up until fourth grade children have worked with angles only when looking at them as part of two-dimensional figures. They recognize "right" angles as square corners, and may have heard the terms "acute" angle (smaller than a right angle) and "obtuse" angle (larger than a right angle). Fourth grade is the first time that children work with angles as shapes themselves. They come to understand an angle *as a figure that is formed at the point where two rays meet.*

In order to determine the measure of angles, fourth graders learn that angles are measured with respect to a circle, where the circle's center is at the point where the two rays meet to form the angle. The outside of every circle is broken into 360 equally-spaced sections called degrees. There are always 360 spaces although in larger circles each space may appear larger than in smaller circles the measure, because it is out of 360-degrees, does not change. Understanding this concept helps children to see that an angle can be measured with any size circle and still have the same measure.

Angle Measurement

Angle(s) – made up of two rays that come from one point known as *the vertex*. Angles are measured using the degrees of a circle (0 to 360), with the number of degrees representing the size of the angle's opening.

Acute angle(s) – all angles measuring less than 90-degrees

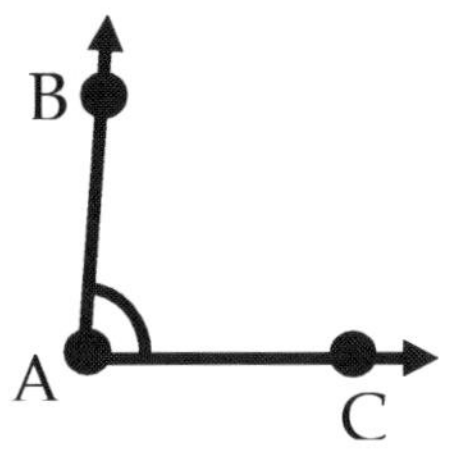

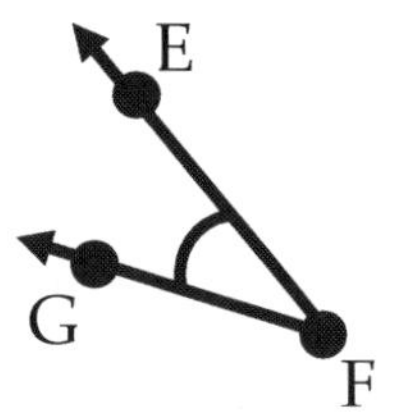

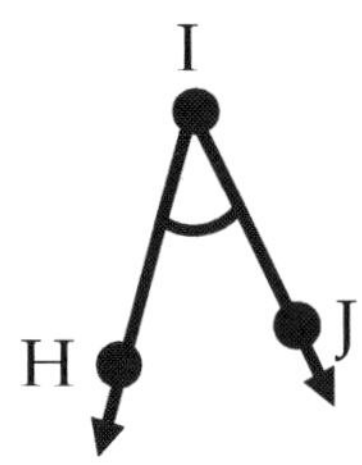

Obtuse angle(s) – all angles measuring greater than 90-degrees

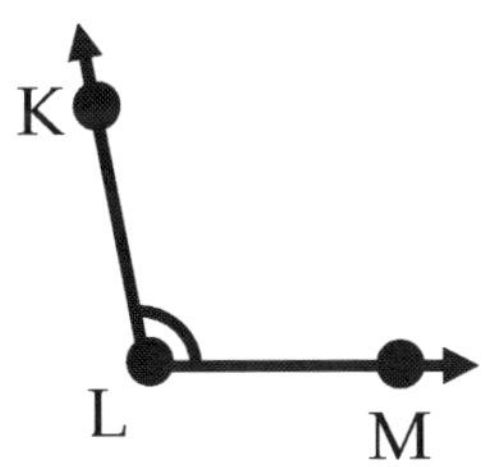

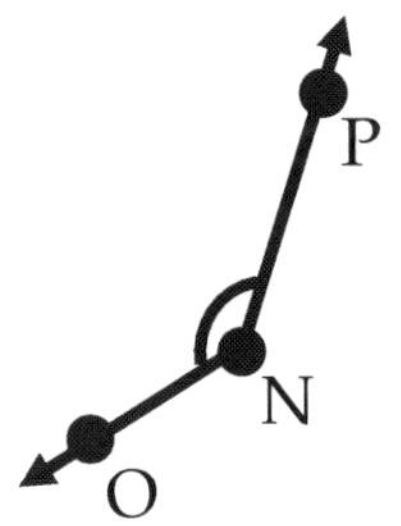

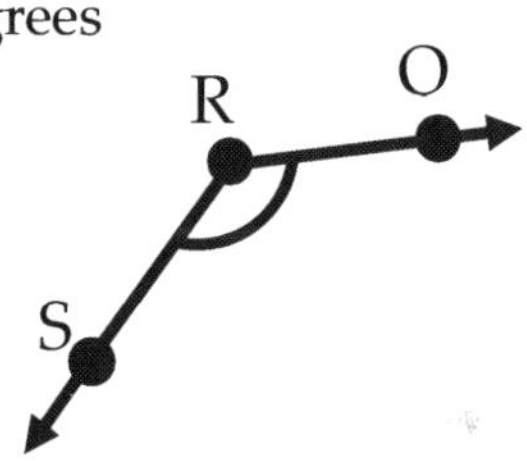

Right angle(s) – any angle measuring EXACTLY 90-degrees

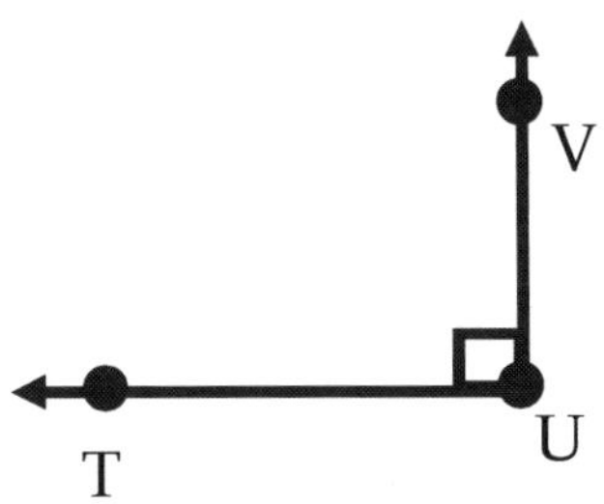

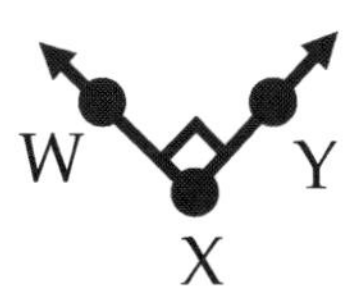

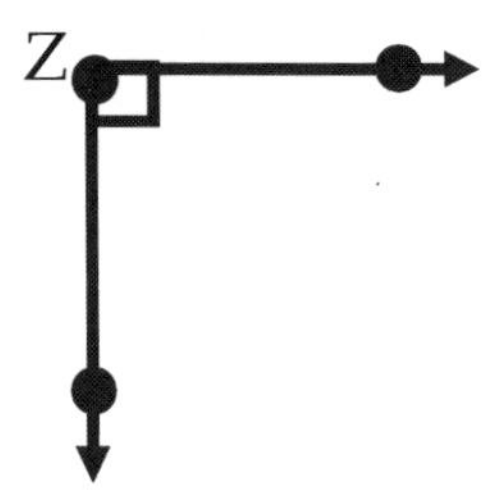

Measuring Angles

Learning standard 4.MD.6 says:

Measure angles in whole-number degrees using a protractor. Sketch angles of specified measure.

What it means:

Children in fourth grade learn how to measure angles using a protractor. They understand that there are two sets of numbers across the top of the protractor, and that they choose which one to use depending on the angle they are measuring.

- Some children might recognize that when they are measuring an angle that is visibly smaller than a right angle, the angle's measure must be less than 90 degrees. Conversely, when an angle is visibly larger than a right angle, the angle must measure more than 90 degrees.

- Some children might look to see which way the angle opens. They know they will use the row of numbers that has "0" on the same side of the protractor as the open side of the angle.

Fourth graders also use protractors to draw angles. When asked to draw an angle of a certain size, first they draw one of the two rays and line up the bottom of the protractor with the ray they drew. After making sure that the bottom center point of the protractor aligns with the vertex (point at which the rays meet - as shown in the diagram on the next page), children mark the spot that matches the number of degrees the angle should measure. Finally, they draw the second ray by connecting the starting point of the first ray with the spot they marked. Children know that the length of the rays doesn't matter; the size of the angle doesn't change even if the lengths of the rays change.

Protractors

Protractor – an instrument used to measure and draw angles. The most commonly used protractors are semi-circular, showing two 0 – 180 degree measurement scales.

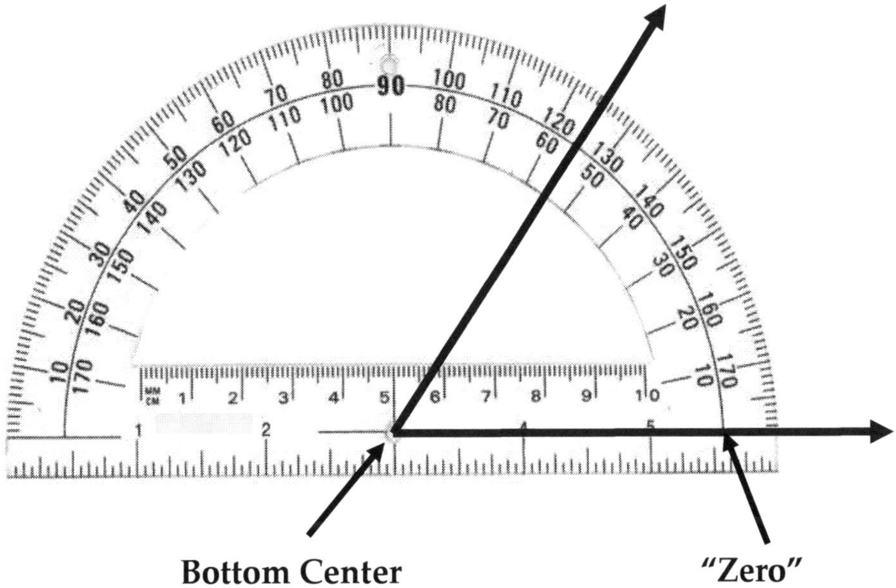

The vertex of the angle (point where the two rays originate) is placed at the bottom center point, with one of the two rays lined up with "zero" degrees. (On protractors where "zero" is not specifically shown, the line even with the center point should be used.)

The place where the second ray crosses the protractor is the angle's measure. (In this example, the angle measures 55 degrees.)

When reading the angle's measure, children need to use their understanding of angle size (greater or less than 90°) to decide which set of numbers to read. (This is an acute angle, so children know to use the measures less than 90 degrees. They understand that it just wouldn't make sense for this angle to measure 125 degrees.)

Using Angle Measurement

Learning standard 4.MD.7 says:

Recognize angle measure as additive. When an angle is decomposed into non-overlapping parts, the angle measure of the whole is the sum of the angle measures of the parts. Solve addition and subtraction problems to find unknown angles on a diagram in real world and mathematical problems, e.g., by using an equation with a symbol for the unknown angle measure.

What it means:

Fourth graders use what they know about angle measurement to solve problems involving the unknown angle sizes. They recognize that when a larger angle is split into smaller parts, the measure of the whole angle is equal to the sum of the smaller angles. In other words, if the measures of all of the smaller angles were added up, they would total the measure of the larger angle.

Children use this concept combined with addition to find the measure of the whole, if they know the size of all of the parts. They can also use subtraction to find the measure of one of the parts if they know the size of the whole and the rest of the parts.

Children also understand that some angles have special relationships. Two angles that form a right angle (have a sum of 90 degrees) are called *complementary angles.* Two angles that form a straight angle (have a sum of 180 degrees) are called *supplementary angles.* Understanding these relationships helps children solve angle measure problems.

Example:

Find the measure of the missing angle.

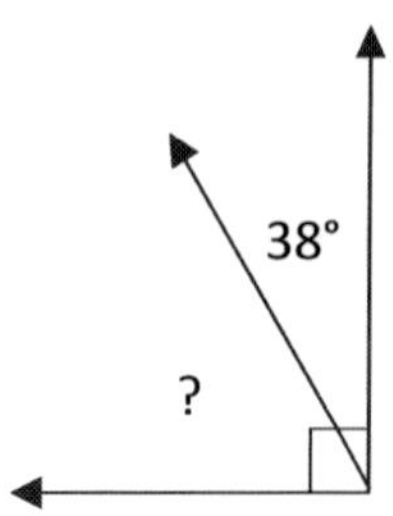

To solve this problem, a child might think, "This whole angle is a right angle, so it equals 90 degrees. Since one part of it is 38 degrees, I can find the measure of the other part if I subtract 90 – 38."

The unknown angle measure is 52°.

Angle Measurement

Complementary angles – two angles that have a sum of 90 degrees (form a right angle). The angles DO NOT have to be "next" to each other.

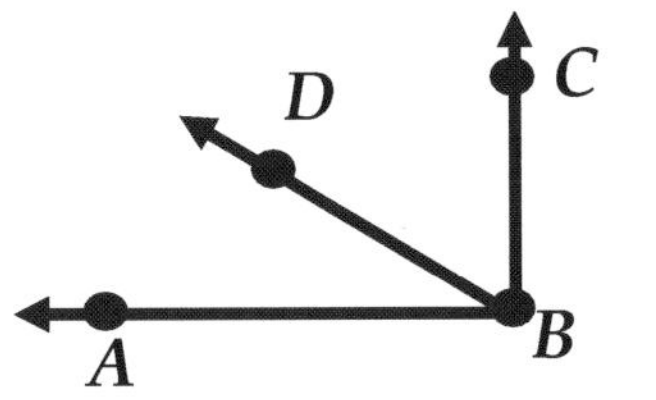

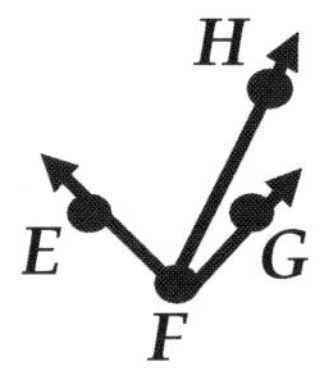

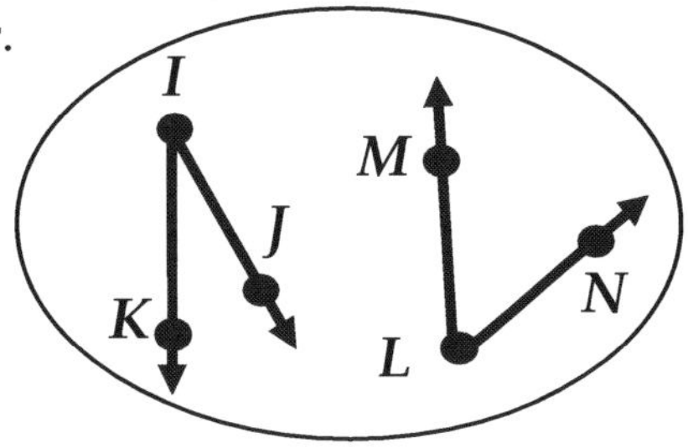

The measures of ∠ ABD and ∠ DBC have a sum of 90° (right ∠ ABC).

The measures of ∠ GFH and ∠ HFE have a sum of 90° (right ∠ EFG).

The measures of ∠ IJK (30-degrees) and ∠ LMN (60-degrees) have a sum of 90°.

Supplementary angles – two angles that have a sum of 180 degrees (form a straight angle). The angles DO NOT have to be "next" to each other.

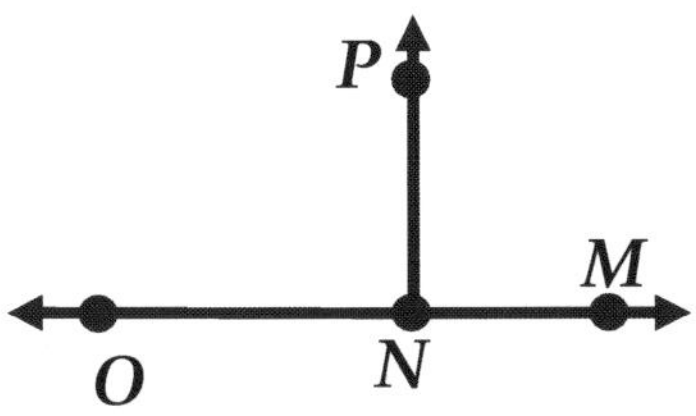

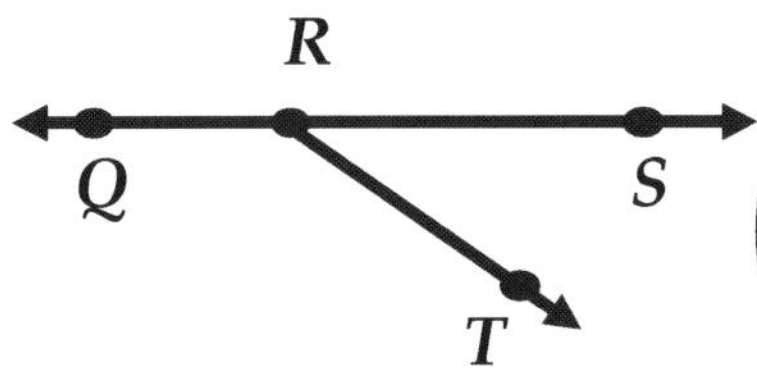

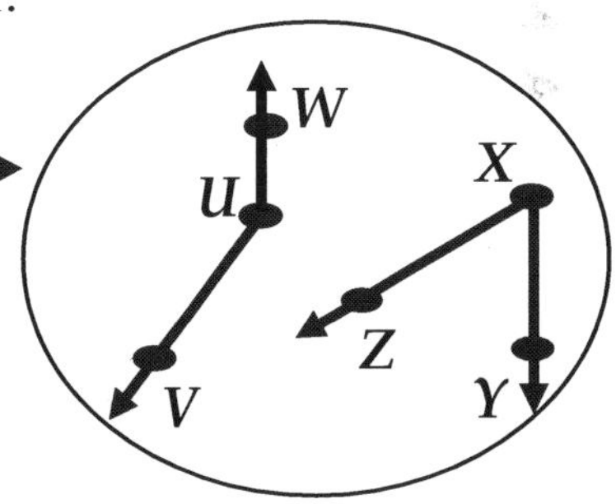

The measures of ∠ ONP and ∠ PNM have a sum of 180 degrees (straight ∠ ONM).

The measures of ∠ QRT and ∠ SRT have a sum of 180 degrees (straight ∠ QRS).

The measures of ∠ UVW (120-degrees) and ∠ XYZ (60-degrees) have a sum of 180 degrees.

GRADE 4- FRACTIONS AND DECIMALS

By meeting the learning standards in this section, fourth grade children will show that they:

Are able to explain why one fraction is equivalent to another fraction.

Are able to compare two fractions with different numerators and different denominators.

Understand that every fraction is made up of unit fractions.

Can add and subtract fractions with the same denominator.

Can multiply a fraction by a whole number.

Are able to use decimal notation for fractions with denominators 10 or 100.

Are able to compare two decimals to hundredths by reasoning about their size.

Important Information about 4th-Grade Fraction Work

It will most likely not surprise a single fourth grade parent to learn that the fraction work fourth graders do looks and feels very different from fractions the way we learned them. While this fact is true for much of the work that is done in grade 4, fractions somehow look even a little "more different". Maybe this is because fractions have traditionally been a tricky topic. Most adults who remember being uncomfortable with math as a child report that fractions was the area that gave them the most trouble.

With all of that in mind, the following points were included here to help you better understand the work you will see throughout this section.

- Fractions "act" like any other numbers. The big difference between fractions and whole numbers is that fractions have two parts. Children understand that the bottom number in a fraction is simply the number of parts "in the whole". So just like $1 + 1 + 1 = 3$, $\frac{1}{4} + \frac{1}{4} + \frac{1}{4} = \frac{3}{4}$. (The 4 in the bottom of the fraction simply tells us that our unit is "fourths", or that the whole has been broken into four equal parts.) Once they understand this simple concept, children are able to work with any fractions.

- All fraction work can be done horizontally. Yes, we mean from left to right. "Stacking fractions" often causes confusion and makes it difficult for children to keep track of what they are doing when solving problems. Throughout this section, the examples that follow each standard will reflect horizontal fraction work. Within each example we have included explanations and arrows to show exactly how it works. Once you get the hang of it, you will see how much sense it makes…and how simple it really can be.

- When most adults were first introduced to fractions, we learned that whenever "the top number was larger than the bottom number the fraction was called IMPROPER". The term "improper fraction" is no longer widely used. The reason for this is simple: It IS possible to have more than 2 halves, or four fourths, etc. Simply having a greater number in the numerator of a fraction doesn't mean there is something "wrong" , as the term "improper" might imply. Many textbook series refer to these fractions as "fractions greater than one". This is also what we have done in this book. Some teachers, and possibly even a few publishers, will still refer to these fractions greater than one as improper. This is OK. The important thing is that you and your child are aware that these terms are interchangeable.

- One last thing that today's adults were taught about fractions is that they must always be "reduced", "simplified" or expressed in "lowest terms". Once again, this is something you will be seeing less and less of. While it is important for children to understand that fractions having equal values can be written using different numbers ($\frac{5}{10} = \frac{1}{2}$), it is NOT always necessary for a fraction to be expressed in its lowest terms. The context of the problem should guide the thinking here. A child who has read 6 chapters of a 12 chapter book, for example, is more likely to state that he has read $\frac{1}{2}$ of the book than $\frac{6}{12}$, even though either would be correct. A child relating four inches to one foot, however, is perfectly correct to state that four inches is $\frac{4}{12}$ of a foot. It is not necessary to express it as $\frac{1}{3}$. Doing so might even be confusing for fourth graders. Some teachers, and possibly even a few publishers, might still teach the skill of simplifying or reducing fractions to students. This is OK. The important thing is that children let the context of a situation dictate when they will and will not simplify a fraction.

Equivalent Fractions

Learning standard 4.NF.1 says:

Explain why a fraction a/b is equivalent to a fraction (n × a)/(n × b) by using visual fraction models, with attention to how the number and size of the parts differ even though the two fractions themselves are the same size. Use this principle to recognize and generate equivalent fractions.

What it means:

In third grade, children worked for the first time with fractions as units of length. They saw that as they created more parts of the same whole (for example creating half- and then quarter- inch segments of the same inch), they were increasing both the denominator and the numerator for fractions that occupied the same point on a number line or ruler (as happened when they determined that $\frac{2}{4}$ and $\frac{1}{2}$ are located at the same spot.)

Fourth graders use this understanding to explore the "fundamental fact about equivalent fractions"… ***the value of a fraction is not changed when the numerator and denominator are multiplied by the same whole number.*** They will practice working with this concept through practice locating fractional points on number lines, and investigating multiple ways to name a single point.

The big idea is that children need to be able to determine when two fractions *are* or *are not* equivalent (even when they look very different). Once this understanding is in place, fourth graders are expected to create equivalent fractions by either multiplying or dividing the numerator and denominator by the same number. Knowledge of basic multiplication and division facts is EXTREMELY helpful here as children "see" the *RELATIONSHIP between both sets* of numerators and denominators.

*Notice in the following examples how the relationship between the fractions helps children determine the missing part.

Example:

What number makes the following equation true?

$$\frac{2}{5} = \frac{?}{15}$$

To solve this problem, a child thinks, "I know that 5 times three is 15. Since the numerator and denominator are multiplied by the same number in equivalent fractions, I am looking for the number that is three times more than 2. The answer is 6."

$$\frac{2}{5} = \frac{6}{15}$$

Example:

What number makes the following equation true?

$$\frac{4}{?} = \frac{24}{36}$$

To solve this problem, a child thinks, "I know that 24 divided by 6 is 4. Since the numerator and denominator are divided by the same number in equivalent fractions, I can divide 36 by 6. The answer is 6."

$$\frac{4}{6} = \frac{24}{36}$$

Example:

Patti completed $\frac{2}{3}$ of her book report. Christopher finished $\frac{8}{12}$ of his report. Christopher said he has more of his report finished than Patti does. Is Christopher correct?

2 x 4

$$\frac{2}{3} = \frac{8}{12}$$

3 x 4

A child answering this question might think, "I need to see if $\frac{2}{3}$ and $\frac{8}{12}$ have the same value."

"Since the numerator and denominator are both multiplied by 4 the fractions are equivalent."

"Christopher is not correct because the fractions have the same value. They both have the same amount done."

Comparing Fractions

Learning standard 4.NF.2 says:

Compare two fractions with different numerators and different denominators, e.g., by creating common denominators or numerators, or by comparing to a benchmark fraction such as 1/2. Recognize that comparisons are valid only when the two fractions refer to the same whole. Record the results of comparisons with symbols >, =, or <, and justify the conclusions, e.g., by using a visual fraction model.

What it means

Understanding that two fractions can have the same value, even when they look different (equivalent fractions) is the foundation fourth grade children build on in order to compare the sizes or values of two different fractions. The big idea is that children determine which of two fractions is greater, and then record the comparison by writing number sentences with the symbols: > (greater than), > (less than), or = (equal to). Since fractions can either look very similar yet have very different values (for example: $\frac{3}{5}$ *and* $\frac{3}{15}$) …or look very different but have the same value (for example: $\frac{2}{4}$ *and* $\frac{5}{10}$), it may not be clear immediately which of two fractions is greater.

To help them compare the values of two fractions fourth graders have a choice of strategies to use:

- Analyzing the relationship between the numerator and denominator.
- Using a number line and "benchmarks" such as $0, \frac{1}{2}$, and 1.
- Creating common denominators
- Creating common numerators

- **Relationship between the Numerator and Denominator:**
  Children in fourth grade know that a fraction is equivalent to one half when the number in the numerator (the top number) is one half of the number in the denominator (the bottom number). For example: $\frac{2}{4}, \frac{3}{6}, \frac{4}{8}, \frac{5}{10}$, etc.... are all equivalent to $\frac{1}{2}$. Children also know that a fraction is equivalent to 1 whole when the numerator and denominator are the same number. For example: $\frac{2}{2}, \frac{3}{3}, \frac{4}{4}, \frac{5}{5}$, etc.... are all equivalent to 1. These two key ideas help children determine which of two fractions is greater, without plotting the fractions on a number line. By reasoning about "how close to each other" the numerators and denominators of the fractions are, children can decide which fraction is greater and which is lesser.

Example:

Compare $\frac{2}{4}$ and $\frac{4}{5}$. Write a number sentence using <, >, or =.

A child using reasoning to solve this problem might think, "Two is half of four, so I know that $\frac{2}{4}$ is equal to one half. In the other fraction, four is greater than half of five. So I know that $\frac{4}{5}$ is greater than one half. That means $\frac{2}{4}$ is less than $\frac{4}{5}$. "

$\frac{2}{4} < \frac{4}{5}$ **(Read left to right as "Two fourths is less than four fifths.")**

Another child solving this problem might reason differently, thinking, "Four is only one away from 5. That means that $\frac{4}{5}$ is almost 1 whole because it only needs one more fifth to be $\frac{5}{5}$. Since $\frac{2}{4}$ is equal to one half, and $\frac{4}{5}$ is almost 1 whole, then $\frac{4}{5}$ is greater than $\frac{2}{4}$.

$\frac{4}{5} > \frac{2}{4}$ **(Read left to right as "Four fifths is greater than two fourths.")**

- **Using Number Lines and Benchmark Fractions:**
  The concepts of "halves" and "quarters" are very well understood by fourth graders. Children can use this understanding in order to determine which of two fractions is greater, by determining which one of them is closer to 1 on a number line. After creating a number line and labeling 0 and 1, children put in markers for "half" and each "quarter" so they can use the number line as a measuring tool. Next children plot the fractions in question on the number line. Based on the positions of the new fractions in relation to the familiar halves and quarters, children are able to determine which is greater.

Example:

Compare $\frac{2}{3}$ and $\frac{3}{8}$. Write a number sentence using <, >, or =.

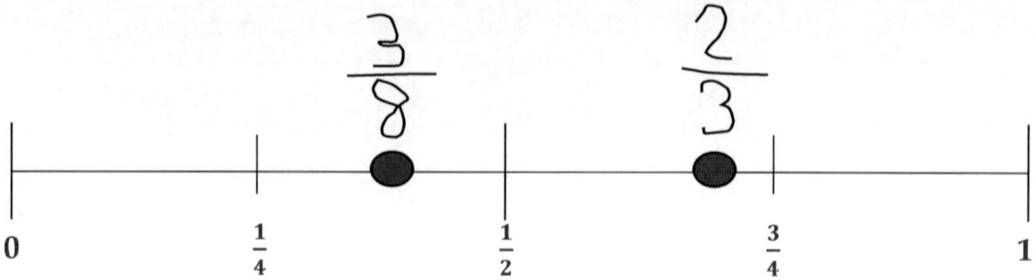

A child using the number line to compare these two fractions might think, "Three eighths has to be less than one half because four eighths would be one half. And I know that two eighths is the same as one fourth. So I can put $\frac{3}{8}$ on the number line between $\frac{1}{2}$ and $\frac{1}{4}$. I know that $\frac{2}{3}$ is greater than one half, so it must also be greater than $\frac{3}{8}$.

$\frac{2}{3} > \frac{3}{8}$ **(Read left to right as "Two thirds is greater than three eighths.")**

- **Creating Common Denominators**:
  Children in fourth grade know that they can change the denominator of a fraction as long as they change the numerator as well (by multiplying or dividing them both by the same number). They understand that this changes the way a fraction looks, but not its value. This understanding allows children to create common denominators in order to determine which of two fractions is greater. Once the denominators are the same the fraction with the larger numerator has a greater value.

Example:

Compare $\frac{2}{3}$ and $\frac{3}{4}$. Write a number sentence using <, >, or =.

In this problem, both fractions are greater than one half, making it difficult for a child to reason it out or use the benchmark and number line strategy.

A child solving it might reason this way, "I can rewrite these fractions to create common denominators. Then the fraction with the greater numerator is the greater fraction."

"If I multiply both parts of $\frac{2}{3}$ by 4, and multiply both parts of $\frac{3}{4}$ by 3, I can make an equivalent fraction for each of them, and the new fractions will both have 12 in the denominator."

2 x 4

$$\frac{2}{3} = \frac{8}{12}$$

3 x 4

3 x 3

$$\frac{3}{4} = \frac{9}{12}$$

4 x 3

"When both fractions have 12 in the denominator, I can see that $\frac{9}{12}$ is greater than $\frac{8}{12}$, so that means $\frac{3}{4}$ is greater than $\frac{2}{3}$

$\frac{3}{4} > \frac{2}{3}$ (Read left to right as "Three fourths is greater than two thirds.")

- **Creating Common Numerators:**
  When two fractions have the same numerator, children know that each fraction represents the same number of parts. When using this information to help them decide which of two fractions is greater, children look at the denominators of each fraction. They know that the fraction with the lesser denominator is the larger fraction since a smaller number in the denominator means that the whole has been divided into fewer parts. Dividing a whole cake into thirds, for example, would create greater size pieces than dividing the same cake into eighths.
  We understand that the high level of reasoning required here is above what most fourth graders can be expected to do! Although some children will "see" this relationship, most won't. This is OK! What IS important here is for children to UNDERSTAND that when fractions have the same numerator they can reason about the fractions' values (compare them) based on the "size" of the denominators. This "common numerators" strategy, in our classrooms, is used only when it "naturally" occurs. It's empowering for children when they see that the numerators of two fractions are the same and they understand what that means. Otherwise, however, we employ the strategy of finding (creating) common denominators.
  The first part of the example on the following page demonstrates how to "make equivalent numerators" while the second example shows how to use this thinking when children are already faced with fractions having common numerators.

Example:

Compare $\frac{2}{3}$ and $\frac{3}{4}$. Write a number sentence using $<$, $>$, or $=$.

In this problem, both fractions are greater than one half, making it difficult for a child to reason it out or use the benchmarks and number line strategy.

A child solving it might reason this way, "I can rewrite these fractions to create common numerators. Then the fraction with the greater denominator is the lesser fraction."

"If I multiply both parts of $\frac{2}{3}$ by 3, and multiply both parts of $\frac{3}{4}$ by 2, I can make an equivalent fraction for each one and both will have 6 as the numerator."

2 x 3

$$\frac{2}{3} = \frac{6}{9}$$

3 x 3

3 x 2

$$\frac{3}{4} = \frac{6}{8}$$

4 x 2

"When both fractions have 6 in the numerator, I can see that $\frac{2}{3}$ is less than $\frac{3}{4}$ because ninths are smaller than eighths. "

$\frac{2}{3} < \frac{3}{4}$ **(Read left to right as "Two thirds is less than three quarters.")**

Example:

$$\frac{5}{8} \bigcirc \frac{5}{9}$$

"When both fractions have 5 in the numerator, I can reason that $\frac{5}{8}$ is greater than $\frac{5}{9}$ because eighths are "bigger pieces" than ninths."

$$\frac{5}{8} \text{ (>) } \frac{5}{9}$$

The big idea here is that children in fourth grade will be exposed to many ways of comparing the size or value of two different fractions. None of these is "the right way", but rather, children learn them all so they will become comfortable enough to use the best one for each comparison situation. Children will discover that some fractions are easy to compare mentally, using what they understand about visualizing and benchmarks. Others may be more difficult to work with mentally and a child may decide to create either common numerators or denominators. Learning all of these strategies is quite helpful for children.

Unit Fractions

Learning standard 4.NF.3 says:

Understand a fraction a/b with a > 1 as a sum of fractions 1/b.
Understand addition and subtraction of fractions as joining and separating parts referring to the same whole.
Decompose a fraction into a sum of fractions with the same denominator in more than one way, recording each decomposition by an equation. Justify decompositions, e.g., by using a visual fraction model. Examples: 3/8 = 1/8 + 1/8 + 1/8 ; 3/8 = 1/8 + 2/8 ; 2 1/8 = 1 + 1 + 1/8 = 8/8 + 8/8 + 1/8.

What it means:

The big idea here is that any fraction is really the sum of unit fractions. This means, for example, that just like 5 = 1 + 1 + 1 + 1 + 1, $\frac{5}{6} = \frac{1}{6} + \frac{1}{6} + \frac{1}{6} + \frac{1}{6} + \frac{1}{6}$. At first look this concept may seem quite simplistic. In fact, you might think you are "missing something". But this simple concept is actually the foundation for fraction operations. Children in fourth grade will add, subtract and begin to multiply fractions. This will all come naturally to them when they understand this concept:

> *Fractions behave the same way whole numbers do. Everything children know and understand about the way whole numbers work applies to their work with fractions.*

This concept also provides a basis for understanding fractions greater than one (also known as "improper" fractions) and mixed numbers.

To understand and practice working with this standard, children demonstrate that they can represent any fraction as the sum of smaller fractions with the same denominator. They write number sentences and create fraction models such as fraction strips or number bonds.

The word "decompose" will often appear in the tasks children complete when learning this concept. Children should remember that *decompose* means to break a number into the sum of its smaller parts. Numbers can be decomposed into many different combinations.

Example:

Decompose $\frac{7}{8}$ into the sum of smaller fractions.

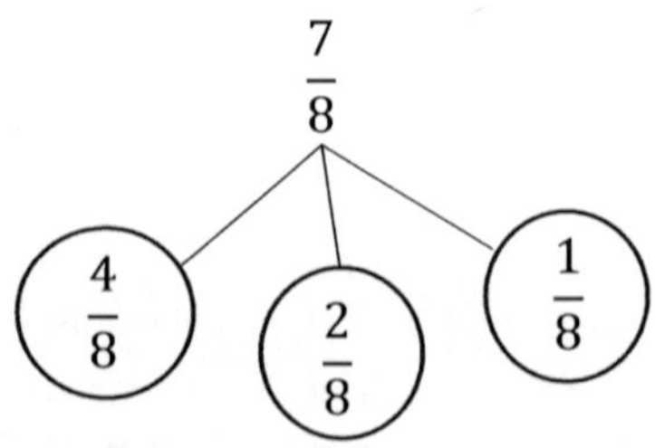

A child solving this problem might use a number bond to show how they can "pull out" smaller parts equal to the total original fraction. Next they use an equation to show that the parts are added together.

$$\frac{7}{8}=\frac{4}{8}+\frac{2}{8}+\frac{1}{8}$$

Another way this child might show the decomposition of this fraction is with a fraction strip.

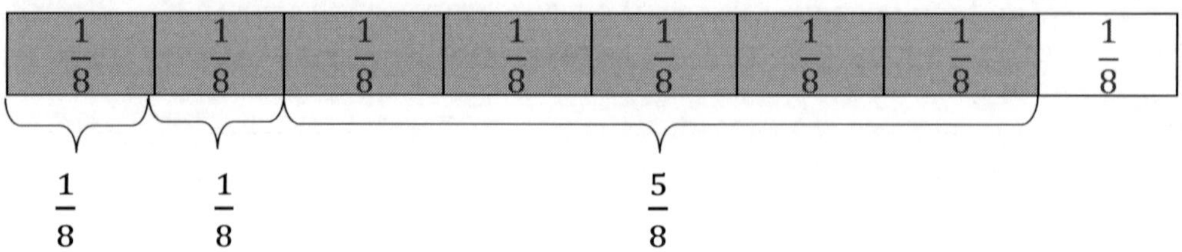

Next he or she would use an equation to show relationship between the original fraction and the parts it was broken into.

$$\frac{1}{8}+\frac{1}{8}+\frac{5}{8}=\frac{7}{8}$$

Example:

Decompose $1\frac{3}{5}$ into the sum of smaller fractions.

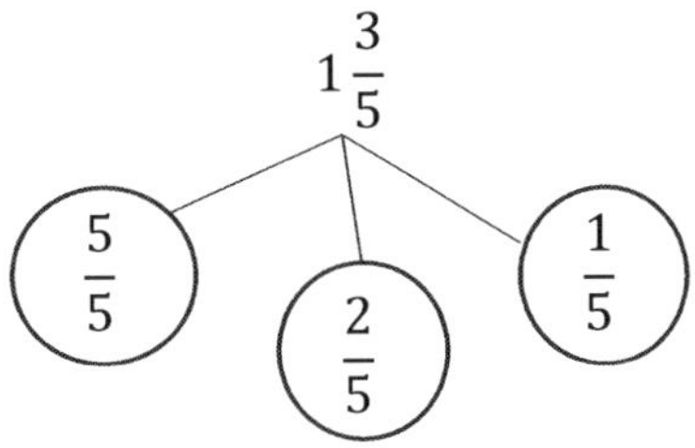

Using a number bond, this child first "pulled out" 1 whole (since $\frac{5}{5}$ is equal to 1). Next he decomposed the fraction, "pulling out" $\frac{2}{5}$ and $\frac{1}{5}$ (to make $\frac{3}{5}$.)

Finally, he used an equation to show the relationship between the original mixed number and the smaller parts.

$$\frac{5}{5}+\frac{2}{5}+\frac{1}{5}=\frac{8}{5}=1\frac{3}{5}$$

Another way this child might show the decomposition of this mixed number is with fraction strips.

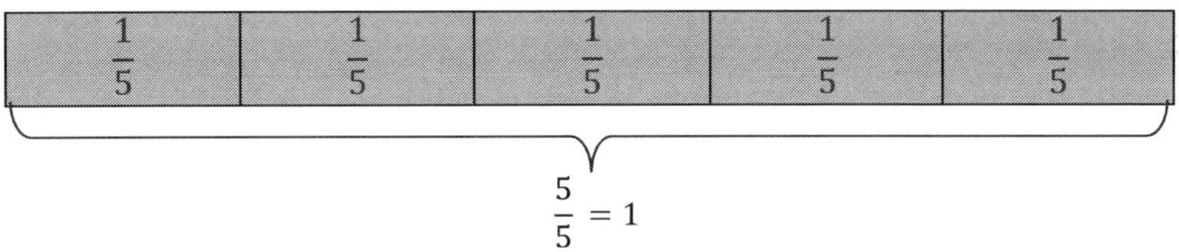

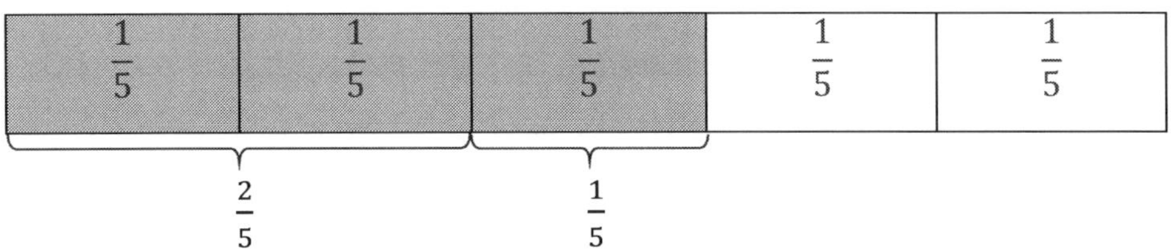

$$\frac{5}{5}+\frac{2}{5}+\frac{1}{5}=\frac{8}{5}=1\frac{3}{5}$$

Adding Fractions and Mixed Numbers

Learning standard 4.NF.3 says:

Understand a fraction a/b with a > 1 as a sum of fractions 1/b.
Add and subtract mixed numbers with like denominators, e.g., by replacing each mixed number with an equivalent fraction, and/or by using properties of operations and the relationship between addition and subtraction.
Solve word problems involving addition and subtraction of fractions referring to the same whole and having like denominators, e.g., by using visual fraction models and equations to represent the problem.

What it means:

Although they have been informally putting fractional parts of objects together to form whole objects since as early as the first grade, children in fourth grade will formally add and subtract fractions for the first time. All of the work they have done decomposing fractions into smaller parts, as well as everything children understand about how numbers work, serves as a foundation for them to add and subtract fractions.

In order to add and subtract fractions, children might use any of these models and/or strategies:

- **Number Lines:**

  The familiar way a number line works allows children to see that **ALL numbers 'ACT' the same way.** Everything they already understand about how a number line works applies to fractions, too!

  - Fractions increase in value as they move to the right on a number line.
  - Fractions decrease in value as they move to the left on a number line

  Using these conventions allows children to visualize fraction addition as "combining", and fraction subtraction as "taking from", in much the same way they do with whole numbers.

When they add and subtract fractions using the number line, children avoid making the very common mistake of adding or subtracting both the top AND bottom numbers in the fractions. Shown this way, that simply doesn't make sense!

Example: **Add** $\frac{4}{5}+\frac{7}{5}$

A child solving this problem knows that the sum of two whole numbers is easily modeled on a number line.

For example: To model the sum 4 + 7, start with 4 and count 7 more steps up to 11, which is the sum.

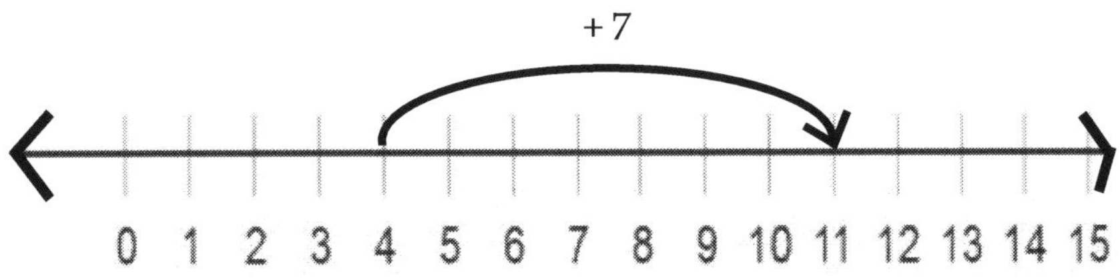

$$\mathbf{4+7=11}$$

To add $\frac{4}{5}+\frac{7}{5}$ this child might use a number line and apply the same reasoning.

He or she starts with $\frac{4}{5}$ and counts 7 more fifths up to $\frac{11}{5}$, which is the sum.

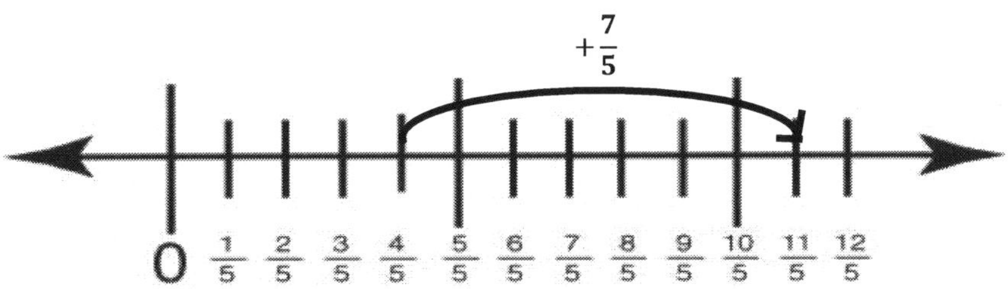

$$\frac{4}{5}+\frac{7}{5}=\frac{11}{5}$$

$$\frac{5}{5} \quad \frac{5}{5} \quad \frac{1}{5}$$

$$\mathbf{1+1+\frac{1}{5}=2\frac{1}{5}}$$

The correct answer can be written either of the ways shown.

Example:

Subtract $\frac{11}{5} - \frac{7}{5}$

A child solving this problem knows that the difference between two whole numbers is easily modeled on a number line.

For example: To model 11 – 7, start with 11 and count back 7 steps to 4, which is the difference.

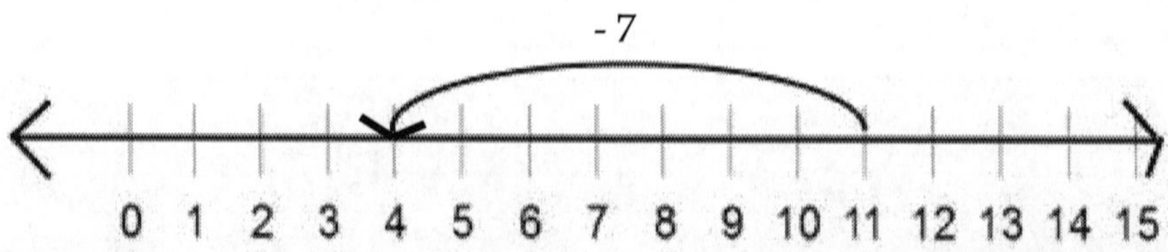

11 - 7 = 4

A child subtracting $\frac{11}{5} - \frac{7}{5}$ might use a number line and apply the same reasoning.

He or she starts with $\frac{11}{5}$ and counts back 7 fifths until they reach $\frac{4}{5}$, which is the difference.

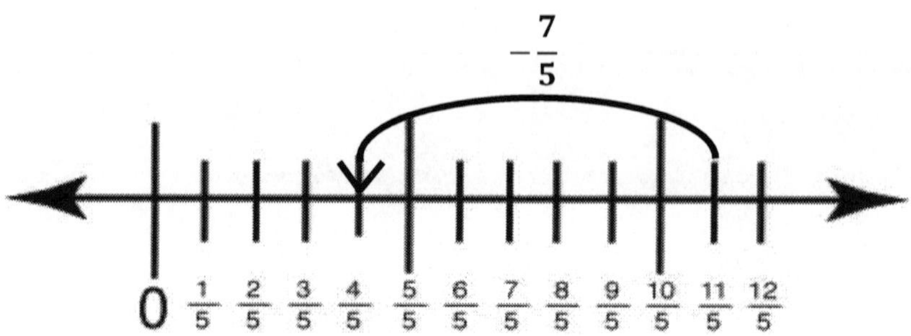

$$\frac{11}{5} - \frac{7}{5} = \frac{4}{5}$$

- **Number Bonds:**
  This model helps children break fractions into smaller parts in order to more easily add or subtract them. This is very similar to what they learned in grade 2 working with whole numbers. When adding, the number bond allows children to "pull out" a part from one fraction in order to make 1 whole. When subtracting, children use number bonds to "break" a whole number into fractional parts in order to be able to subtract the fractions.

Example:

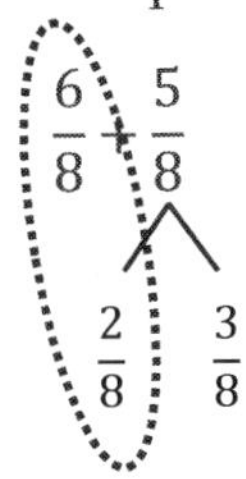

$$\frac{8}{8}+\frac{3}{8}=1+\frac{3}{8}=1\frac{3}{8}$$

To solve this problem, a child might use what they know about number bonds and combining fractions to make 1 whole. He or she might think, "Six eighths only needs two more eighths to make one whole. I can use a number bond to pull out $\frac{2}{8}$ from $\frac{5}{8}$, leaving $\frac{3}{8}$. Then I can combine $\frac{6}{8}$ and $\frac{2}{8}$ to make 1 whole.

Finally I just have to add 1 and $\frac{3}{8}$."

In this problem, a number bond was used to help with addition. The child solving the problem used it to "pull out" the additional parts they needed to make a whole.

Example:

$$2\frac{2}{5} - \frac{4}{5}$$

When a child first looks at this problem, he or she might think, "I can't subtract $\frac{4}{5}$ from $\frac{2}{5}$, but I can use a number bond to "pull out" some more fifths from 2.

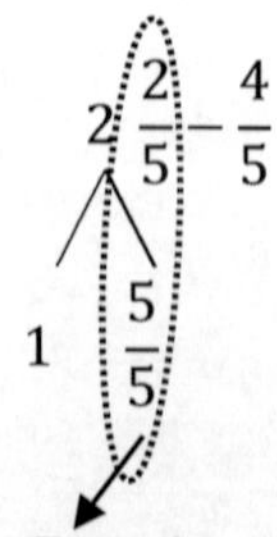

$$1\frac{7}{5} - \frac{4}{5} = 1\frac{3}{5}$$

Next, he or she might think, "After I use the number bond to decompose 2 into 1 and $\frac{5}{5}$, I just combine the $\frac{5}{5}$ with the $\frac{2}{5}$ …that makes the problem $1\frac{7}{5} - \frac{4}{5}$. Now it's easy!"

To finish the problem he or she reasons, "Seven minus four is three, so $\frac{7}{5} - \frac{4}{5}$ is $\frac{3}{5}$. Since nothing is being subtracted from the 1, the answer is $1\frac{3}{5}$.

In this problem, a number bond was used to help with subtraction. The child solving the problem used it to "pull out" the additional parts they needed to be able to subtract the fractions.

Multiplying Fractions by Whole Numbers

Learning standard 4.NF.4 says:

Apply and extend previous understandings of multiplication to multiply a fraction by a whole number
Understand a fraction a/b as a multiple of 1/b. For example, use a visual fraction model to represent 5/4 as the product 5 × (1/4), recording the conclusion by the equation 5/4 = 5 × (1/4)
Understand a multiple of a/b as a multiple of 1/b, and use this understanding to multiply a fraction by a whole number. For example, use a visual fraction model to express 3 × (2/5) as 6 × (1/5), recognizing this product as 6/5. (In general, n × (a/b) = (n × a)/b.)
Solve word problems involving multiplication of a fraction by a whole number, e.g., by using visual fraction models and equations to represent the problem. For example, if each person at a party will eat 3/8 of a pound of roast beef, and there will be 5 people at the party, how many pounds of roast beef will be needed? Between what two whole numbers does your answer lie?

What it means:

Fourth graders initially learned the concept of multiplication as "repeated addition". They learned, for example, that "5 x 2" is the same as "5 groups of 2", which is also the same as "2 + 2 + 2 + 2 + 2". Children in fourth grade will use this concept, along with their understanding of fraction addition, as a foundation for multiplying a whole number and a fraction.

The goal is for children to understand that when they are multiplying a whole number by a fraction, the whole number actually tells how many times the fraction is being added to itself. This means that "$5 \times \frac{1}{2}$" is the same as "5 groups of $\frac{1}{2}$", which is also the same as "$\frac{1}{2}+\frac{1}{2}+\frac{1}{2}+\frac{1}{2}+\frac{1}{2}$" or $\frac{5}{2}$. (Children know from their work with fraction addition that the denominator doesn't change.)

The big idea here is for children to "discover" that when they multiply a whole number by a fraction, they can simply multiply the whole number by the numerator of the fraction, and keep the denominator the same. By discovering this "shortcut" on their own, AFTER they understand the reasoning, children are much more likely to remember this concept.

Example:

$$4 \times \frac{2}{3}$$

One child solving this problem might use a fraction model to represent it, thinking, "This problem is the same as finding 4 groups of $\frac{2}{3}$. So I can draw 4 fraction bars showing $\frac{2}{3}$. Then I can count all of the shaded thirds to find the answer."

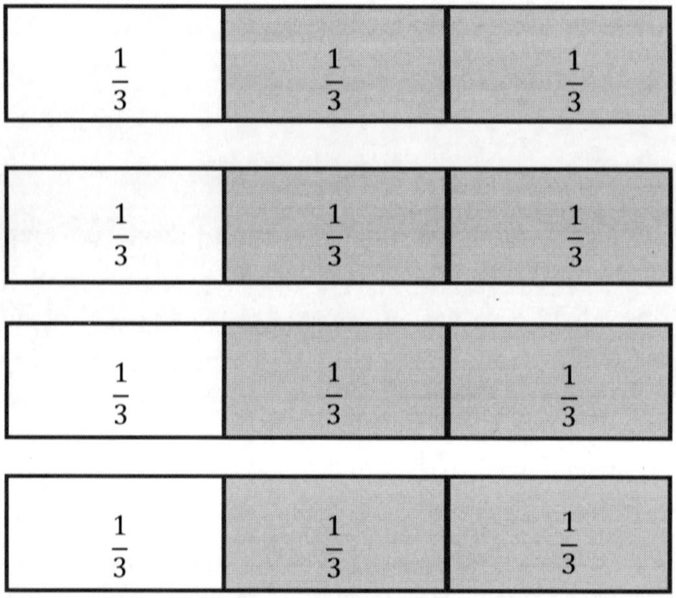

"There are 8 thirds shaded…so 4 groups of $\frac{2}{3}$ is $\frac{8}{3}$. I can write the equation:

$$4 \times \frac{2}{3} = \frac{8}{3}$$

Another child solving the same problem might simply reason this way, "Since I know that I am making four groups of two thirds, I can multiply 4 x 2 to get the new numerator, and keep 3 in the denominator. So: $4 \times \frac{2}{3} = \frac{8}{3}$."

Example:

Solve the following problem by creating a fraction model and writing an equation.

The local butcher sold 8 packages of ground beef in one day. Each package weighed $\frac{3}{4}$ of a pound. How many pounds of ground beef did the butcher sell?

To solve this problem, a child thinks, "I need to create a fraction model that shows 8 copies of $\frac{3}{4}$."

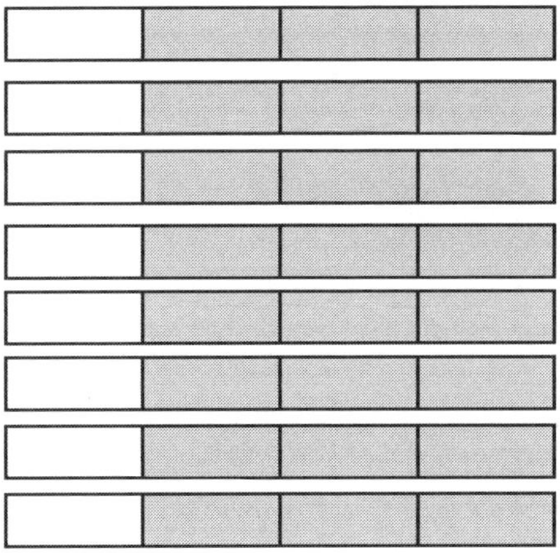

He or she then goes on to reason, "Since the butcher sold 8 packages with $\frac{3}{4}$ of a pound in each one, I need to multiply 8 x $\frac{3}{4}$."

8 x $\frac{3}{4}$ is the same as 8 groups of $\frac{3}{4}$, which is also the same as $\frac{3}{4}+\frac{3}{4}+\frac{3}{4}+\frac{3}{4}+\frac{3}{4}+\frac{3}{4}+\frac{3}{4}+\frac{3}{4}$,

so $8\ x\ \frac{3}{4}=\frac{24}{4}$.

**At this point in their work with fractions, many children will recognize that $\frac{24}{4}=6$. Children are considered correct whether they convert the answer to the whole number or leave it as a fraction.*

Relating Tenths and Hundredths

Learning standard 4.NF.5 says:

Express a fraction with denominator 10 as an equivalent fraction with denominator 100, and use this technique to add two fractions with respective denominators 10 and 100.[2] For example, express 3/10 as 30/100, and add 3/10 + 4/100 = 34/100.

What it means:

Fourth grade children use what they understand about creating equivalent fractions in order to express a fraction with a denominator of 10 as an equivalent fraction with a denominator of 100. (For example, children know that by multiplying both the numerator and denominator by 10, they can express $\frac{3}{10}$ as $\frac{30}{100}$.) They know that any fraction can be changed in appearance by multiplying the numerator and denominator by the same number. Changing the "look" of the fraction in this way doesn't change its "value".

This understanding is used by children in order to add tenths and hundredths. This is the first time children in fourth grade add fractions having different denominators, but it is a simple transition for them. They are quick to see that after representing tenths as hundredths they can add the fractions easily.

Example:

$$\frac{7}{10} + \frac{6}{100}$$

A child solving this problem might think, "If I try to add these fractions the way they are it doesn't make sense. I can't add them because they don't show the same units. Tenths and hundredths are different sizes. The denominators need to be the same so that when I add the numerators I get a total number of the same unit."

"I can change $\frac{7}{10}$ into an equal amount of hundredths. If I multiply the numerator and denominator by 10, it becomes $\frac{70}{100}$. Now I can add the fractions."

$$\frac{70}{100} + \frac{6}{100} = \frac{76}{100}$$

Understanding Decimals

Learning standard 4.NF.6 says:

Use decimal notation for fractions with denominators 10 or 100. For example, rewrite 0.62 as 62/100; describe a length as 0.62 meters; locate 0.62 on a number line diagram.

What it means:

Children in fourth grade use their understanding of fractions to work with decimals for the first time. They learn to read decimal numbers the same way they read fractions.

For example:

2.3 means $2\frac{3}{10}$ and is read as "two and three tenths"

.23 means $\frac{23}{100}$ and is read as "twenty-three hundredths"

Children also learn that tenths and hundredths written in decimal form have the same meaning as tenths and hundredths written as fractions.

So:

$$2.3 = 2.30 \quad \text{because} \quad 2\frac{3}{10} = 2\frac{30}{100}$$

A place value chart is often used to model the reason decimal numbers look the way they do. Children in fourth grade develop a deep understanding of place value, and they recognize that each place in the chart is ten times greater than the place to its right. (As a child moves to the right on a place value chart they see, for example, that 1 thousand is the same as 10 hundreds…1 hundred is the same as 10 tens…1 ten is the same as 10 ones…so it makes sense the 1 one is the same as 10 tenths…and 1 tenth is the same as 1 hundredth…) Using this reasoning they are able to determine that the place to the right of the ones column must be equal to one-tenth of one.

This understanding helps correct the common misconception that there is a "oneths" place. Children come to understand that the ones column on the place value chart is the center of the chart (NOT the decimal point*). Once they see the ones place as the center, it makes sense to them that "the place value rule of 10" means there are tens on one side of the ones, and tenths on the other.

**The "job" of the decimal point is simply to separate the "whole" numbers from the "parts of numbers".*

Example:

Write seven hundredths in both fraction and decimal form.

A child answering this question might reason, "Hundredths is the name of the unit, and there are seven of them. To make that a fraction I make the numerator 7, and the denominator 100."

$$\frac{7}{100}$$

To write the decimal form, he or she might continue, "I need to write the number of hundredths in the hundredths place. There are no "wholes" so I can start with a zero, and then write a decimal point before I write the parts. The first place after the decimal point is the tenths place, so I need to put a zero there, too. If I don't put a zero in the tenths place, the seven will look like it is in the wrong spot. Then I can put the seven in the hundredths place."

Hundreds	Tens	Ones	Tenths	Hundredths
		0	0	7

0.07

**This problem represents a common trouble spot for children. When they are writing single-digit hundredths (like the seven hundredths in this problem) they have little difficulty writing the fraction, but often forget that they need to place the single-digit in the hundredths place when writing the decimal form. Placing the digit in the hundredths place requires children to also place a zero in the tenths place, as this place can't be left empty. Children are familiar with this concept when writing whole numbers (they know, for example that the number three hundred five, 305, needs a zero in the tens place). This is the understanding we should point out to children who may be "forgetting to hold the tenths place" with a zero in problems like this one. Showing them how this work connects to what they already understand will make it easier for them to do.*

Example:

Write three and seventeen hundredths in both fraction and decimal form.

When answering this question a child would likely think, "Three and seventeen hundreds contains "wholes" and "parts". So in fraction form I will need a whole number and a fraction."

$$3\frac{17}{100}$$

In decimal form I need a numbers on both sides of the decimal point. The "wholes" go on the left side, and the "parts" go on the right side."

$$3.17$$

Comparing Decimals

Learning standard 4.NF.7 says:

Compare two decimals to hundredths by reasoning about their size. Recognize that comparisons are valid only when the two decimals refer to the same whole. Record the results of comparisons with the symbols >, =, or <, and justify the conclusions, e.g., by using a visual model.

What it means:

Children in fourth grade work with number comparisons throughout the year. They compare whole numbers, fractions, and now decimal numbers using reasoning. Working with decimals, children write comparison number sentences containing <, >, or = symbols, just like they did with whole numbers and fractions. The meaning of the symbols is the same, only the appearance of the numbers they are working with has changed. This allows fourth graders to rely on what they already know in order to do this work.

Decimal comparison is often a simple concept for children. There is, however, one common sticking point. A mistake many children make is thinking that a greater number of hundredths is greater than a lesser number of tenths. For example…thinking that 0.42 is greater than 0.6. At first glance this seems so simple, because with whole numbers 42 is indeed greater than 6. Teachers and parents use various strategies to correct this. Any strategy that helps children understand this concept is great! One that works very well is to have children read the two decimal numbers aloud. If they say two different units (as they would in this case with "42 hundredths" and "6 tenths") they should be reminded that they *can't compare the size of different units*. They can then restate them both as hundredths. When children hear themselves say "42 hundredths" and "60 hundredths", they will instantly see the greater one. Writing each decimal number in a place value chart is also helpful.

Example:

Compare 0.68 and 0.7. Write a number sentence using <, > or = to record your comparison.

Hundreds	Tens	Ones	Tenths	Hundredths
		0	6	8
		0	8	0

When a child uses a place value chart to compare these two decimal numbers, and represents "eight tenths" as "eighty hundredths", it makes it easy to see which of the two is greater.

0.68 < 0.80

"Sixty-eight hundredths is less than eighty hundredths."

Example:

Compare 0.4 and 0.40. Write a number sentence using <, > or = to record your comparison.

Hundreds	Tens	Ones	Tenths	Hundredths
		0	4	0
		0	4	0

0.4 = 0.40

GRADE 4- FRACTION AND DECIMAL MODELS

Number Line

Number Bonds

Fraction Bars (Strips)

Fraction/decimal equivalence

Write the decimal equivalent of each fraction (decimal fractions).

$\frac{3}{10} =$

$\frac{3}{100} =$

Read each fraction (three tenths; three hundredths) and use a place value chart to show the decimal equivalence (decimal fractions).

hundreds	tens	ones		tenths	hundredths
			•	3	
			•	0	3

$\frac{3}{10} = 0.3$

$\frac{3}{100} = 0.03$

Fractions on a number line or ruler

Using *benchmarks* to compare fractions

(*The dotted lines above and below each number line are used to show how a ruler might look.)

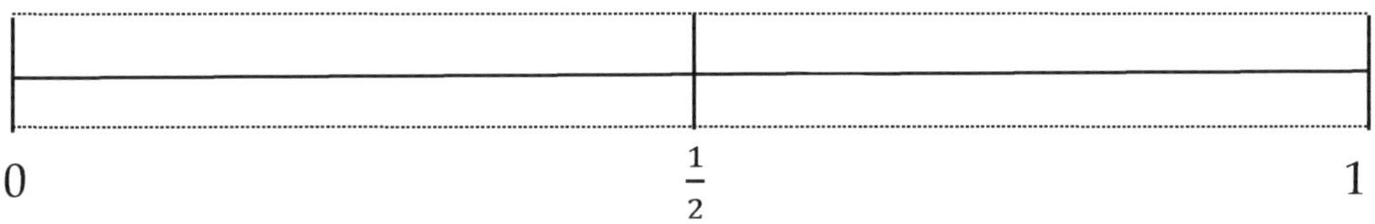

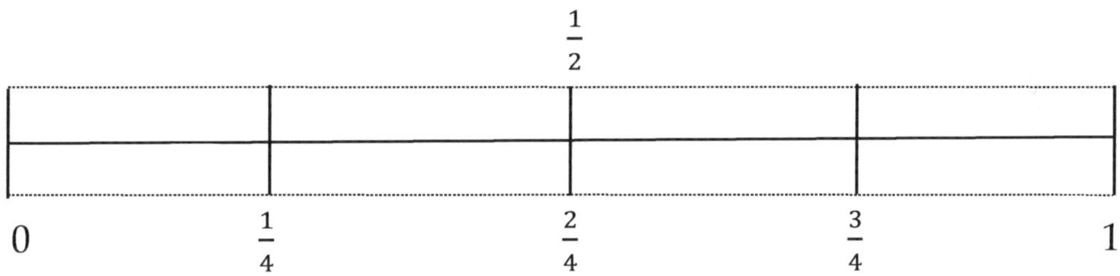

1 x 2

$\frac{1}{2} = \frac{2}{4}$

2 x 2

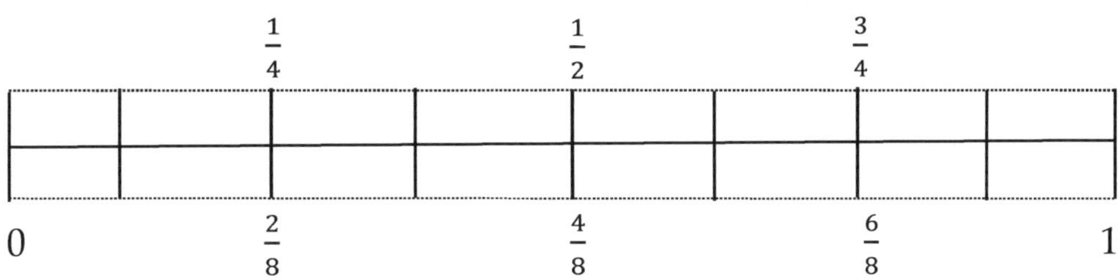

1 x 2	1 x 4	3 x 2
$\frac{1}{4} = \frac{2}{8}$	$\frac{1}{2} = \frac{4}{8}$	$\frac{3}{4} = \frac{6}{8}$
4 x 2	2 x 4	4 x 2

Comparing fractions using benchmarks, and equivalence on a number line

$\frac{3}{8} \bigcirc \frac{5}{6}$

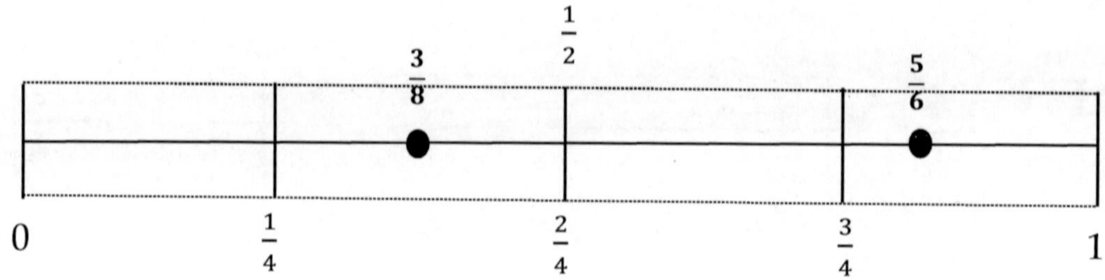

Using $\frac{1}{2}$ as a benchmark to "place" fractions on a number line.

With a denominator of 8 and a numerator of 3 we know that it is less than half (because 4 is half of 8). We also know that $\frac{1}{4} = \frac{2}{8}$, so $\frac{3}{8}$ is between $\frac{1}{4}$ and $\frac{1}{2}$. The fraction $\frac{5}{6}$ is almost 1 whole so we place it close to 1. Eventually children will move away from placing the fractions on a number line and simply use this reasoning.

GRADE 4- DATA COLLECTION AND MODELS

By meeting the learning standards in this section, fourth grade children will show that they:

Are able to make a line plot to display measurements in increments of $\frac{1}{2}$, $\frac{1}{4}$, ***and*** $\frac{1}{8}$.

(Can create a line plot to represent a set of measurement data.)

Can solve addition and subtraction word problems based on the information presented in line plots.

(Know how to interpret the data displayed on a line plot in order to solve word problems.)

Creating Line Plots

Standard 4.MD.4 says:

Make a line plot to display a data set of measurements in fractions of a unit (1/2, 1/4, 1/8). Solve problems involving addition and subtraction of fractions by using information presented in line plots. For example, from a line plot find and interpret the difference in length between the longest and shortest specimens in an insect collection.

What it means:

In third grade children measured groups of objects to the nearest $\frac{1}{4}$, $\frac{1}{2}$, or whole inch. They also recorded their measurements to make *a set of data,* and then *created a line plot to display their data.* Fourth graders continue working with measurement data sets and line plots, extending the concept to include measurements to the nearest $\frac{1}{8}$ of a unit. A line plot starts as a number line, with the numbers written under the marks. X's are placed above the number marks to represent the pieces of data (the measurements). One X is used to represent one piece of data.

It's important that the X's placed in the line plot are the same size and that they're spaced evenly.

*Notice that the intervals on the line plot in the following example are all expressed in terms of eighths. Using the same fraction across the line plot helps children create equal intervals. When measuring items to collect their data, however, children may use half- and quarter-inch fractions. Most children will realize that they must convert all of their measurements to eighths in order to plot the data. ($\frac{1}{2}$ for example, will need to be plotted as $\frac{4}{8}$.) Some may need to be reminded that they should use what they know about creating equivalent fractions in order to complete this task.

Example:

Measure the length of 10 crayons to the nearest $\frac{1}{8}$ inch. Create a line plot to display your data set.

A child might create a line plot like the one below to complete this task:

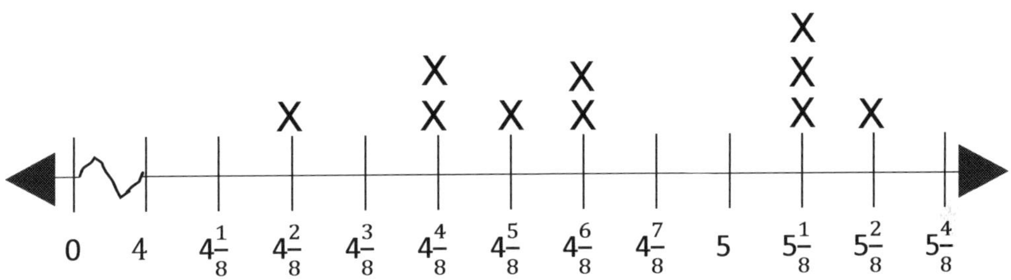

It is important for the interval (the space between the numbers), in this case $\frac{1}{8}$ of an inch, to be equally-spaced across the line plot.

One X in this case represents one crayon, making it easy to see from this line plot that more $5\frac{1}{8}$ inch crayons were measured than any other size. Data represented on a line plot is generally easy for children to interpret.

Children can use the information in this graph to answer questions such as:

- What is the length of crayon that appeared the most? How many crayons are there at that length?
- What is the length of the shortest crayon that you measured? How many are there at that length?
- What is the length of the longest crayon that you measured? How many are there?
- How many crayons measured between $4\frac{5}{8}$ and $5\frac{1}{8}$ inches long?
- Are there more crayons less than 5 inches long, or more than 5 inches long? How many more?

NOTES

NOTES

65730194R10087

Made in the USA
Lexington, KY
23 July 2017